Accession no.

KU-743-387

SARAH KANE

Blasted

with commentary and notes by
KEN URBAN

LIS - LIBRARY

Date	Fund
4|6|18	xl-Shr

Order No.

02876346

University of Chester

Bloomsbury Methuen Drama
An imprint of Bloomsbury Publishing Plc

BLOOMSBURY
LONDON · OXFORD · NEW YORK · NEW DELHI · SYDNEY

Bloomsbury Methuen Drama

An imprint of Bloomsbury Publishing Plc

Imprint previously known as Methuen Drama

50 Bedford Square	1385 Broadway
London	New York
WC1B 3DP	NY 10018
UK	USA

www.bloomsbury.com

BLOOMSBURY, METHUEN DRAMA and the Diana logo are trademarks of Bloomsbury Publishing Plc

Blasted first published in 1995 by Methuen in *Frontline Intelligence 2*
This edition first published in the United Kingdom in 2011 by
Bloomsbury Methuen Drama
Reprinted 2013, 2014, 2016, 2017

© Sarah Kane, 1995
Commentary and notes © Methuen Drama, 2011

Sarah Kane and Ken Urban have asserted their rights under the Copyright,
Designs and Patents Act, 1988, to be identified as authors of this work.

All rights reserved. No part of this publication may be reproduced or transmitted in
any form or by any means, electronic or mechanical, including photocopying,
recording, or any information storage or retrieval system, without prior
permission in writing from the publishers.

No responsibility for loss caused to any individual or organization acting on or
refraining from action as a result of the material in this publication can be
accepted by Bloomsbury or the author.

All rights whatsoever in this play are strictly reserved and application for performance etc. should
be made before rehearsals by professionals and by amateurs to Casarotto Ramsay & Associates Ltd,
Waverley House, 7–12 Noel Street, London W1F 8GQ Mail to: rights@casarotto.co.uk.
No performance may be given unless a licence has been obtained.

No rights in incidental music or songs contained in the work are hereby granted
and performance rights for any performance/presentation whatsoever
must be obtained from the respective copyright owners.

British Library Cataloguing-in-Publication Data
A catalogue record for this book is available from the British Library.

ISBN: PB: 978-1-4081-0385-2

Library of Congress Cataloging-in-Publication Data
A catalog record for this book is available from the Library of Congress.

Series: Student Editions

Typeset by Country Setting, Kingsdown, Kent
Printed and bound in Great Britain

Contents

Sarah Kane: 1971–1999   v

BLASTED   1

Commentary   63
  'This disgusting feast of filth'   64
  Blasted and new writing in the 1990s   67
  Borrowing from the past   79
  The logic of war   85
  The universal: Kane, Pinter and Beckett   91
  The logic of rape   93
  The violence of men   97
  The possibility of ethics   101
  Cate's gift   106
  Conclusion   108

Notes to Commentary   109
Further Reading   114
Acting Exercises   117
Questions for Further Study   119

Sarah Kane: 1971–1999

January 1995   *Blasted*, Royal Court Theatre Upstairs

May 1996   *Phaedra's Love*, Gate Theatre

June 1997   *Skin*, Channel 4

April 1998   *Cleansed*, Royal Court Theatre Downstairs

August 1998   *Crave*, Traverse Theatre

June 2000   *4.48 Psychosis*, Royal Court Jerwood Theatre Upstairs

Blasted

For Vincent O'Connell, with thanks.

Blasted was first performed at the Royal Court Theatre Upstairs, London, on 12 January 1995. The cast was as follows:

Ian	Pip Donaghy
Cate	Kate Ashfield
Soldier	Dermot Kerrigan

Directed by James Macdonald
Designed by Franziska Wilcken
Lighting by Jon Linstrum
Sound by Paul Arditti

Characters

Ian
Cate
Soldier

Author's note

Punctuation is used to indicate delivery, not to conform to the rules of grammar.

A stroke (/) marks the point of interruption in overlapping dialogue.

Words in square brackets [ ] are not spoken, but have been included in the text to clarify meaning.

Stage directions in brackets ( ) function as lines.

Editor's note

This edition of *Blasted*, first reprinted in 2000, incorporates minor revisions made to the original text by Sarah Kane shortly before her death. It should therefore be regarded as the definitive version in all respects.

Scene One

A very expensive hotel room in Leeds – the kind that is so expensive it could be anywhere in the world.

There is a large double bed.
A mini-bar and champagne on ice.
A telephone.
A large bouquet of flowers.
Two doors – one is the entrance from the corridor, the other leads off to the bathroom.

Two people enter – **Ian** *and* **Cate**.

Ian *is 45, Welsh born but lived in Leeds much of his life and picked up the accent.*

Cate *is 21, a lower-middle-class Southerner with a south London accent and a stutter when under stress.*

They enter.

Cate *stops at the door, amazed at the classiness of the room.*
Ian *comes in, throws a small pile of newspapers on the bed, goes straight to the mini-bar and pours himself a large gin.*
He looks briefly out of the window at the street, then turns back to the room.

Ian   I've shat in better places than this.

(He gulps down the gin.)

I stink.
You want a bath?

Cate   *(Shakes her head.)*

Ian *goes into the bathroom and we hear him run the water. He comes back in with only a towel around his waist and a revolver in his hand. He checks it is loaded and puts it under his pillow.*

Ian   Tip that wog when he brings up the sandwiches.

He leaves fifty pence and goes into the bathroom.
Cate *comes further into the room.*
She puts her bag down and bounces on the bed.
She goes around the room, looking in every drawer, touching everything.
She smells the flowers and smiles.

Cate   Lovely.

Ian *comes back in, hair wet, towel around his waist, drying himself off.*
He stops and looks at **Cate** *who is sucking her thumb.*
He goes back in the bathroom where he dresses.
We hear him coughing terribly in the bathroom.
He spits in the sink and re-enters.

Cate   You all right?

Ian   It's nothing.

He pours himself another gin, this time with ice and tonic, and sips it at a more normal pace.
He collects his gun and puts it in his under-arm holster.
He smiles at **Cate**.

Ian   I'm glad you've come. Didn't think you would.

(*He offers her champagne.*)

Cate   (*Shakes her head.*)

I was worried.

Ian   This? (*He indicates his chest.*) Don't matter.

Cate   I didn't mean that. You sounded unhappy.

Ian   (*Pops the champagne. He pours them both a glass.*)

Cate   What we celebrating?

Ian   (*Doesn't answer. He goes to the window and looks out.*)

Hate this city. Stinks. Wogs and Pakis taking over.

Cate   You shouldn't call them that.

Ian Why not?

Cate It's not very nice.

Ian You a nigger-lover?

Cate Ian, don't.

Ian You like our coloured brethren?

Cate Don't mind them.

Ian Grow up.

Cate There's Indians at the day centre where my brother goes. They're really polite.

Ian So they should be.

Cate He's friends with some of them.

Ian Retard, isn't he?

Cate No, he's got learning difficulties.

Ian Aye. Spaz.

Cate No he's not.

Ian Glad my son's not a Joey.

Cate Don't c- call him that.

Ian Your mother I feel sorry for. Two of you like it.

Cate Like wh- what?

Ian (*Looks at her, deciding whether or not to continue. He decides against it.*)

You know I love you.

Cate (*Smiles a big smile, friendly and non-sexual.*)

Ian Don't want you ever to leave.

Cate I'm here for the night.

Ian   (*Drinks.*)

Sweating again. Stink. You ever thought of getting married?

Cate   Who'd marry me?

Ian   I would.

Cate   I couldn't.

Ian   You don't love me. I don't blame you, I wouldn't.

Cate   I couldn't leave Mum.

Ian   Have to one day.

Cate   Why?

Ian   (*Opens his mouth to answer but can't think of one.*)

There is a knock at the door.
Ian *starts, and* **Cate** *goes to answer it.*

Ian   Don't.

Cate   Why not?

Ian   I said.

He takes his gun from the holster and goes to the door.
He listens.
Nothing.

Cate   (*Giggles.*)

Ian   Shh.

He listens.
Still nothing.

Ian   Probably the wog with the sarnies. Open it.

Cate *opens the door.*
There's no one there, just a tray of sandwiches on the floor.
She brings them in and examines them.

Cate   Ham. Don't believe it.

Ian   (*Takes a sandwich and eats it.*)

Champagne?

Cate   (*Shakes her head.*)

Ian   Got something against ham?

Cate   Dead meat. Blood. Can't eat an animal.

Ian   No one would know.

Cate   No, I can't, I actually can't, I'd puke all over the place.

Ian   It's only a pig.

Cate   I'm hungry.

Ian   Have one of these.

Cate   I CAN'T.

Ian   I'll take you out for an Indian.
Jesus, what's this? Cheese.

> **Cate** *beams.*
> *She separates the cheese sandwiches from the ham ones, and eats.*
> **Ian** *watches her.*

Ian   Don't like your clothes.

Cate   (*Looks down at her clothes.*)

Ian   You look like a lesbos.

Cate   What's that?

Ian   Don't look very sexy, that's all.

Cate   Oh.

(*She continues to eat.*)

Don't like your clothes either.

Ian   (*Looks down at his clothes.*
Then gets up, takes them all off and stands in front of her, naked.)

Put your mouth on me.

Cate   (*Stares. Then bursts out laughing.*)

Ian   No?
Fine.
Because I stink?

Cate   (*Laughs even more.*)

> **Ian** *attempts to dress, but fumbles with embarrassment.*
> *He gathers his clothes and goes into the bathroom where he dresses.*
> **Cate** *eats, and giggles over the sandwiches.*
> **Ian** *returns, fully dressed.*
> *He picks up his gun, unloads and reloads it.*

Ian   You got a job yet?

Cate   No.

Ian   Still screwing the taxpayer.

Cate   Mum gives me money.

Ian   When are you going to stand on your own feet?

Cate   I've applied for a job at an advertising agency.

Ian   (*Laughs genuinely.*)

No chance.

Cate   Why not?

Ian   (*Stops laughing and looks at her.*)

Cate. You're stupid. You're never going to get a job.

Cate   I am. I am not.

Ian   See.

Cate   St- Stop it. You're doing it deliberately.

Ian   Doing what?

Cate   C- Confusing me.

Ian   No, I'm talking, you're just too thick to understand.

Cate I am not, I am not.

> **Cate** *begins to tremble.* **Ian** *is laughing.*
> **Cate** *faints.*
> **Ian** *stops laughing and stares at her motionless body.*

Ian Cate?

> (*He turns her over and lifts up her eyelids.*
> *He doesn't know what to do.*
> *He gets a glass of gin and dabs some on her face.*)

Cate (*Sits bolt upright, eyes open but still unconscious.*)

Ian Fucking Jesus.

Cate (*Bursts out laughing, unnaturally, hysterically, uncontrollably.*)

Ian Stop fucking about.

Cate (*Collapses again and lies still.*)

> **Ian** *stands by helplessly.*
> *After a few moments,* **Cate** *comes round as if waking up in the morning.*

Ian What the Christ was that?

Cate Have to tell her.

Ian Cate?

Cate She's in danger.

> (*She closes her eyes and slowly comes back to normal.*
> *She looks at* **Ian** *and smiles.*)

Ian What now?

Cate Did I faint?

Ian That was real?

Cate Happens all the time.

Ian What, fits?

Cate   Since Dad came back.

Ian   Does it hurt?

Cate   I'll grow out of it the doctor says.

Ian   How do you feel?

Cate   (*Smiles.*)

Ian   Thought you were dead.

Cate   [I] Suppose that's what it's like.

Ian   Don't do it again, fucking scared me.

Cate   Don't know much about it, I just go. Feels like I'm
away for minutes or months sometimes, then I come
back just where I was.

Ian   It's terrible.

Cate   I didn't go far.

Ian   What if you didn't come round?

Cate   Wouldn't know. I'd stay there.

Ian   Can't stand it.

(*He goes to the mini-bar and pours himself another large gin and
lights a cigarette.*)

Cate   What?

Ian   Death. Not being.

Cate   You fall asleep and then you wake up.

Ian   How do you know?

Cate   Why don't you give up smoking?

Ian   (*Laughs.*)

Cate   You should. They'll make you ill.

Ian   Too late for that.

Cate Whenever I think of you it's with a cigarette and a gin.

Ian Good.

Cate They make your clothes smell.

Ian Don't forget my breath.

Cate Imagine what your lungs must look like.

Ian Don't need to imagine. I've seen.

Cate When?

Ian Last year. When I came round, surgeon brought in this lump of rotting pork, stank. My lung.

Cate He took it out?

Ian Other one's the same now.

Cate But you'll die.

Ian Aye.

Cate Please stop smoking.

Ian Won't make any difference.

Cate Can't they do something?

Ian No. It's not like your brother, look after him he'll be all right.

Cate They die young.

Ian I'm fucked.

Cate Can't you get a transplant?

Ian Don't be stupid. They give them to people with a life. Kids.

Cate People die in accidents all the time, they must have some spare.

Ian Why? What for? Keep me alive to die of cirrhosis in three months' time.

Cate   You're making it worse, speeding it up.

Ian   Enjoy myself while I'm here.

(He inhales deeply on his cigarette and swallows the last of the gin neat.)

[I'll] Call that coon, get some more sent up.

Cate   *(Shakes.)*

Ian   Wonder if the conker understands English.

*He notices **Cate**'s distress and cuddles her.*
He kisses her.
She pulls away and wipes her mouth.

Cate   Don't put your tongue in, I don't like it.

Ian   Sorry.

*The telephone rings loudly. **Ian** starts, then answers it.*

Ian   Hello?

Cate   Who is it?

Ian   *(Covers the mouthpiece.)* Shh.

(Into the mouthpiece.) Got it here.

(He takes a notebook from the pile of newspapers and dictates down the phone.)

A serial killer slaughtered British tourist Samantha Scrace, S – C – R – A – C – E, in a sick murder ritual comma, police revealed yesterday point new par. The bubbly nineteen year old from Leeds was among seven victims found buried in identical triangular tombs in an isolated New Zealand forest point new par. Each had been stabbed more than twenty times and placed face down comma, hands bound behind their backs point new par. Caps up, ashes at the site showed the maniac had stayed to cook a meal, caps down point new par. Samantha comma, a beautiful redhead with dreams of becoming a model comma, was on the trip of a lifetime after finishing her A levels last year point. Samantha's heartbroken mum said yesterday colon quoting, we pray the police will come up with something dash, anything comma, soon point still quoting. The sooner this lunatic is brought to justice the better point end quote new par. The Foreign Office warned tourists Down Under to take extra care point. A spokesman said colon quoting, common sense is the best rule point end quote, copy ends.

(*He listens. Then he laughs.*)

Exactly.

(*He listens.*)

That one again, I went to see her. Scouse tart, spread her legs. No. Forget it. Tears and lies, not worth the space.

(*He presses a button on the phone to connect him to room service.*)

Tosser.

Cate How do they know you're here?

Ian Told them.

Cate Why?

Ian In case they needed me.

Cate Silly. We came here to be away from them.

Ian Thought you'd like this. Nice hotel.

(*Into the mouthpiece.*)

Bring a bottle of gin up, son.

(*He puts the phone down.*)

Cate We always used to go to yours.

Ian That was years ago. You've grown up.

Cate   (*Smiles.*)

Ian   I'm not well any more.

Cate   (*Stops smiling.*)

Ian kisses her.
She responds.
He puts his hand under her top and moves it towards her breast.
With the other hand he undoes his trousers and starts masturbating.
He begins to undo her top.
She pushes him away.

Cate   Ian, d- don't.

Ian   What?

Cate   I don't w- want to do this.

Ian   Yes you do.

Cate   I don't.

Ian   Why not? You're nervous, that's all.

(*He starts to kiss her again.*)

Cate   I t- t- t- t- t- t- t- told you. I really like you but I
c- c- c- c- can't do this.

Ian   (*Kissing her.*) Shhh.

(*He starts to undo her tr*   )

Cate *panics.*
She starts to tremble   articulate crying sounds.
Ian *stops, fright   ng another 'fit' on.*

Ian   All rig   all right. We don't have to do
any

He strokes   ace until she has calmed down.
She sucks her thumb.
Then.

Ian   That wasn't very fair.

Cate   What?

Ian   Leaving me hanging, making a prick of myself.

Cate   I f- f- felt –

Ian   Don't pity me, Cate. You don't have to fuck me 'cause I'm dying, but don't push your cunt in my face then take it away 'cause I stick my tongue out.

Cate   I- I- Ian.

Ian   What's the m- m- matter?

Cate   I k- k- kissed you, that's all. I l- l- like you.

Ian   Don't give me a hard-on if you're not going to finish me off. It hurts.

Cate   I'm sorry.

Ian   Can't switch it on and off like that. If I don't come my cock aches.

Cate   I didn't mean it.

Ian   Shit. (*He appears to be in considerable pain.*)

Cate   I'm sorry. I am. I won't do it again.

> **Ian**, *apparently still in pain, takes her hand and grasps it around his penis, keeping his own hand over the top.*
> *Like this, he masturbates until he comes with some genuine pain.*
> *He releases* **Cate***'s hand and she withdraws it.*

Cate   Is it better?

Ian   (*Nods.*)

Cate   I'm sorry.

Ian   Don't worry. Can we make love tonight?

Cate   No.

Ian   Why not?

Cate   I'm not your girlfriend any more.

Ian   Will you be my girlfriend again?

Cate   I can't.

Ian   Why not?

Cate   I told Shaun I'd be his.

Ian   Have you slept with him?

Cate   No.

Ian   Slept with me before. You're more mine than his.

Cate   I'm not.

Ian   What was that about then, wanking me off?

Cate   I d- d- d- d-

Ian   Sorry. Pressure, pressure. I love you, that's all.

Cate   You were horrible to me.

Ian   I wasn't.

Cate   Stopped phoning me, never said why.

Ian   It was difficult, Cate.

Cate   Because I haven't got a job?

Ian   No, pet, not that.

Cate   Because of my brother?

Ian   No, no, Cate. Leave it now.

Cate   That's not fair.

Ian   I said leave it.

(*He reaches for his gun.*)

There is a knock at the door.
Ian *starts, then goes to answer it.*

Ian   I'm not going to hurt you, just leave it. And keep quiet. It'll only be Sooty after something.

Cate   Andrew.

Ian   What do you want to know a conker's name for?

Cate   I thought he was nice.

Ian   After a bit of black meat, eh? Won't do it with me but you'll go with a whodat.

Cate   You're horrible.

Ian   Cate, love, I'm trying to look after you. Stop you getting hurt.

Cate   You hurt me.

Ian   No, I love you.

Cate   Stopped loving me.

Ian   I've told you to leave that.
Now.

He kisses her passionately, then goes to the door.
When his back is turned, **Cate** *wipes her mouth.*
Ian *opens the door. There is a bottle of gin outside on a tray.*
Ian *brings it in and stands, unable to decide between gin and champagne.*

Cate   Have champagne, better for you.

Ian   Don't want it better for me.

(*He pours himself a gin.*)

Cate   You'll die quicker.

Ian   Thanks. Don't it scare you?

Cate   What?

Ian   Death.

Cate   Whose?

Ian   Yours.

Cate   Only for Mum. She'd be unhappy if I died. And my brother.

Ian   You're young.
When I was your age –
Now.

Cate   Will you have to go to hospital?

Ian   Nothing they can do.

Cate   Does Stella know?

Ian   What would I want to tell her for?

Cate   You were married.

Ian   So?

Cate   She'd want to know.

Ian   So she can throw a party at the coven.

Cate   She wouldn't do that. What about Matthew?

Ian   What about Matthew?

Cate   Have you told him?

Ian   I'll send him an invite for the funeral.

Cate   He'll be upset.

Ian   He hates me.

Cate   He doesn't.

Ian   He fucking does.

Cate   Are you upset?

Ian   Yes. His mother's a lesbos. Am I not preferable to that?

Cate   Perhaps she's a nice person.

Ian   She don't carry a gun.

Cate   I expect that's it.

Ian   I loved Stella till she became a witch and fucked off with
a dyke, and I love you, though you've got the potential.

Cate   For what?

Ian   Sucking gash.

Cate   (*Utters an inarticulate sound.*)

Ian   You ever had a fuck with a woman?

Cate   No.

Ian   You want to?

Cate   Don't think so. Have you? With a man.

Ian   You think I'm a cocksucker? You've seen me. (*He vaguely
indicates his groin.*) How can you think that?

Cate   I don't. I asked. You asked me.

Ian   You dress like a lesbos. I don't dress like a cocksucker.

Cate   What do they dress like?

Ian   Hitler was wrong about the Jews who have they hurt the
queers he should have gone for scum them and the wogs
and fucking football fans send a bomber over Elland
Road finish them off.

(*He pours champagne and toasts the idea.*)

Cate   I like football.

Ian   Why?

Cate   It's good.

Ian   And when was the last time you went to a football
match?

Cate   Saturday. United beat Liverpool 2–0.

Ian   Didn't you get stabbed?

Cate   Why should I?

Ian   That's what football's about. It's not fancy footwork and scoring goals. It's tribalism.

Cate   I like it.

Ian   You would. About your level.

Cate   I go to Elland Road sometimes. Would you bomb me?

Ian   What do you want to ask a question like that for?

Cate   Would you though?

Ian   Don't be thick.

Cate   But would you?

Ian   Haven't got a bomber.

Cate   Shoot me, then. Could you do that?

Ian   Cate.

Cate   Do you think it's hard to shoot someone?

Ian   Easy as shitting blood.

Cate   Could you shoot me?

Ian   Could you shoot me stop asking that could you shoot me you could shoot me.

Cate   I don't think so.

Ian   If I hurt you.

Cate   Don't think you would.

Ian   But if.

Cate   No, you're soft.

Ian   With people I love.

   (*He stares at her, considering making a pass.*)

Cate   (*Smiles at him, friendly.*)

Ian   What's this job, then?

Cate Personal Assistant.

Ian Who to?

Cate Don't know.

Ian Who did you write the letter to?

Cate Sir or madam.

Ian You have to know who you're writing to.

Cate It didn't say.

Ian How much?

Cate What?

Ian Money. How much do you get paid.

Cate Mum said it was a lot. I don't mind about that as long as I can go out sometimes.

Ian Don't despise money. You got it easy.

Cate I haven't got any money.

Ian No and you haven't got kids to bring up neither.

Cate Not yet.

Ian Don't even think about it. Who would have children. You have kids, they grow up, they hate you and you die.

Cate I don't hate Mum.

Ian You still need her.

Cate You think I'm stupid. I'm not stupid.

Ian I worry.

Cate Can look after myself.

Ian Like me.

Cate No.

Ian You hate me, don't you.

Cate   You shouldn't have that gun.

Ian   May need it.

Cate   What for?

Ian   (*Drinks.*)

Cate   Can't imagine it.

Ian   What?

Cate   You. Shooting someone. You wouldn't kill anything.

Ian   (*Drinks.*)

Cate   Have you ever shot anyone?

Ian   Your mind.

Cate   Have you though?

Ian   Leave it now, Cate.

She takes the warning.
Ian *kisses her and lights a cigarette.*

Ian   When I'm with you I can't think about anything else. You take me to another place.

Cate   It's like that when I have a fit.

Ian   Just you.

Cate   The world don't exist, not like this.
Looks the same but –
Time slows down.
A dream I get stuck in, can't do nothing about it.
One time –

Ian   Make love to me.

Cate   Blocks out everything else.
Once –

Ian   [I'll] Make love to you.

Cate   It's like that when I touch myself.

Ian *is embarrassed.*

Cate Just before I'm wondering what it'll be like, and just after I'm thinking about the next one, but just as it happens it's lovely, I don't think of nothing else.

Ian Like the first cigarette of the day.

Cate That's bad for you though.

Ian Stop talking now, you don't know anything about it.

Cate Don't need to.

Ian Don't know nothing. That's why I love you, want to make love to you.

Cate But you can't.

Ian Why not?

Cate I don't want to.

Ian Why did you come here?

Cate You sounded unhappy.

Ian Make me happy.

Cate I can't.

Ian Please.

Cate No.

Ian Why not?

Cate Can't.

Ian Can.

Cate How?

Ian You know.

Cate Don't.

Ian Please.

Cate No.

Ian   I love you.

Cate   I don't love you.

Ian   (*Turns away. He sees the bouquet of flowers and picks it up.*)

These are for you.

Blackout.

The sound of spring rain.

Scene Two

The same.

Very early the following morning.
Bright and sunny – it's going to be a very hot day.
The bouquet of flowers is now ripped apart and scattered around the room.

Cate *is still asleep.*
Ian *is awake, glancing through the newspapers.*

Ian *goes to the mini-bar. It is empty.*
He finds the bottle of gin under the bed and pours half of what is left into a glass.
He stands looking out of the window at the street.
He takes the first sip and is overcome with pain.
He waits for it to pass, but it doesn't. It gets worse.
Ian *clutches his side – it becomes extreme.*
He begins to cough and experiences intense pain in his chest, each cough tearing at his lung.

Cate *wakes and watches* **Ian**.

Ian *drops to his knees, puts the glass down carefully, and gives in to the pain.*
It looks very much as if he is dying.
His heart, lung, liver and kidneys are all under attack and he is making involuntary crying sounds.

Just at the moment when it seems he cannot survive this, it begins to ease.
Very slowly, the pain decreases until it has all gone.

Ian *is a crumpled heap on the floor.*

He looks up and sees **Cate** *watching him.*

Cate   Cunt.

Ian   (*Gets up slowly, picks up the glass and drinks.*
He lights his first cigarette of the day.)

I'm having a shower.

Cate   It's only six o'clock.

Ian   Want one?

Cate   Not with you.

Ian   Suit yourself. Cigarette?

Cate   (*Makes a noise of disgust.*)

They are silent.

Ian *stands, smoking and drinking neat gin.*
When he's sufficiently numbed, he comes and goes between the bedroom and bathroom, undressing and collecting discarded towels.
He stops, towel around his waist, gun in hand, and looks at **Cate**.
She is staring at him with hate.

Ian   Don't worry, I'll be dead soon.

(*He tosses the gun onto the bed.*)

Have a pop.

Cate *doesn't move.*
Ian *waits, then chuckles and goes into the bathroom.*
We hear the shower running.

Cate *stares at the gun.*
She gets up very slowly and dresses.
She packs her bag.
She picks up **Ian**'s *leather jacket and smells it.*

She rips the arms off at the seams.
She picks up his gun and examines it.
We hear **Ian** *coughing up in the bathroom.*
Cate *puts the gun down and he comes in.*
He dresses.
He looks at the gun.

Ian   No?

(*He chuckles, unloads and reloads the gun and tucks it in his holster.*)

We're one, yes?

Cate   (*Sneers.*)

Ian   We're one.
Coming down for breakfast? It's paid for.

Cate   Choke on it.

Ian   Sarky little tart this morning, aren't we?

He picks up his jacket and puts one arm through a hole.
He stares at the damage, then looks at **Cate**.
A beat, then she goes for him, slapping him around the head hard and fast.
He wrestles her onto the bed, her still kicking, punching and biting.
She takes the gun from his holster and points it at his groin.
He backs off rapidly.

Ian   Easy, easy, that's a loaded gun.

Cate   I d- d- d- d- d- d- d- d- d-

Ian   Catie, come on.

Cate   d- d- d- d- d- d- d- d- d- d-

Ian   You don't want an accident. Think about your mum.
And your brother. What would they think?

Cate   I d- d- d- d- d- d- d- d- d- d- d- d- d-

Cate *trembles and starts gasping for air.*
She faints.

Ian *goes to her, takes the gun and puts it back in the holster.*
Then lies her on the bed on her back.
He puts the gun to her head, lies between her legs, and simulates sex.
As he comes, **Cate** *sits bolt upright with a shout.*
Ian *moves away, unsure what to do, pointing the gun at her from behind.*
She laughs hysterically, as before, but doesn't stop.
She laughs and laughs and laughs until she isn't laughing any more, she's crying her heart out.
She collapses again and lies still.

Ian   Cate? Catie?

Ian *puts the gun away.*
He kisses her and she comes round.
She stares at him.

Ian   You back?

Cate   Liar.

Ian *doesn't know if this means yes or no, so he just waits.*
Cate *closes her eyes for a few seconds, then opens them.*

Ian   Cate?

Cate   Want to go home now.

Ian   It's not even seven. There won't be a train.

Cate   I'll wait at the station.

Ian   It's raining.

Cate   It's not.

Ian   Want you to stay here. Till after breakfast at least.

Cate   No.

Ian   Cate. After breakfast.

Cate   No.

Ian   (*Locks the door and pockets the key.*)

I love you.

Cate   I don't want to stay.

Ian   Please.

Cate   Don't want to.

Ian   You make me feel safe.

Cate   Nothing to be scared of.

Ian   I'll order breakfast.

Cate   Not hungry.

Ian   (*Lights a cigarette.*)

Cate   How can you smoke on an empty stomach?

Ian   It's not empty. There's gin in it.

Cate   Why can't I go home?

Ian   (*Thinks.*)

It's too dangerous.

Outside, a car backfires – there is an enormous bang.
Ian *throws himself flat on the floor.*

Cate   (*Laughs.*)

It's only a car.

Ian   You. You're fucking thick.

Cate   I'm not. You're scared of things when there's nothing to be scared of. What's thick about not being scared of cars?

Ian   I'm not scared of cars. I'm scared of dying.

Cate   A car won't kill you. Not from out there.
Not unless you ran out in front of it.

(*She kisses him.*)

What's scaring you?

Ian   Thought it was a gun.

Cate   (*Kisses his neck.*)

Who'd have a gun?

Ian   Me.

Cate   (*Undoes his shirt.*)

You're in here.

Ian   Someone like me.

Cate   (*Kisses his chest.*)

Why would they shoot at you?

Ian   Revenge.

Cate   (*Runs her hands down his back.*)

Ian   For things I've done.

Cate   (*Massages his neck.*)

Tell me.

Ian   Tapped my phone.

Cate   (*Kisses the back of his neck.*)

Ian   Talk to people and I know I'm being listened to. I'm
sorry I stopped calling you but –

Cate   (*Strokes his stomach and kisses between his shoulder blades.*)

Ian   Got angry when you said you loved me, talking soft on
the phone, people listening to that.

Cate   (*Kisses his back.*)

Tell me.

Ian   In before you know it.

Cate   (*Licks his back.*)

Ian   Signed the Official Secrets Act, shouldn't be telling you
this.

Cate   (*Claws and scratches his back.*)

Ian Don't want to get you into trouble.

Cate (*Bites his back.*)

Ian Think they're trying to kill me. Served my purpose.

Cate (*Pushes him onto his back.*)

Ian Done the jobs they asked. Because I love this land.

Cate (*Sucks his nipples.*)

Ian Stood at stations, listened to conversations and given the nod.

Cate (*Undoes his trousers.*)

Ian Driving jobs. Picking people up, disposing of bodies, the lot.

Cate (*Begins to perform oral sex on* **Ian**.)

Ian Said you were dangerous.

So I stopped.

Didn't want you in any danger.

But

Had to call you again

Missed

This

Now

I do

The real job

I

Am

A

Killer

On the word 'killer' he comes.
As soon as **Cate** *hears the word she bites his penis as hard as she can.*
Ian*'s cry of pleasure turns into a scream of pain.*
He tries to pull away but **Cate** *holds on with her teeth.*
He hits her and she lets go.
Ian *lies in pain, unable to speak.*
Cate *spits frantically, trying to get every trace of him out of her mouth.*
She goes to the bathroom and we hear her cleaning her teeth.
Ian *examines himself. He is still in one piece.*
Cate *returns.*

Cate   You should resign.

Ian   Don't work like that.

Cate   Will they come here?

Ian   I don't know.

Cate   (*Begins to panic.*)

Ian   Don't start that again.

Cate   I c- c- c- c- c-

Ian   Cate, I'll shoot you myself you don't stop.
I told you because I love you, not to scare you.

Cate   You don't.

Ian   Don't argue I do. And you love me.

Cate   No more.

Ian   Loved me last night.

Cate   I didn't want to do it.

Ian   Thought you liked that.

Cate   No.

Ian   Made enough noise.

Cate   It was hurting.

Ian Went down on Stella all the time, didn't hurt her.

Cate You bit me. It's still bleeding.

Ian Is that what this is all about?

Cate You're cruel.

Ian Don't be stupid.

Cate Stop calling me that.

Ian You sleep with someone holding hands and kissing you wank me off then say we can't fuck get into bed but don't want me to touch you what's wrong with you Joey?

Cate I'm not. You're cruel. I wouldn't shoot someone.

Ian Pointed it at me.

Cate Wouldn't shoot.

Ian It's my job. I love this country. I won't see it destroyed by slag.

Cate It's wrong to kill.

Ian Planting bombs and killing little kiddies, that's wrong. That's what they do. Kids like your brother.

Cate It's wrong.

Ian Yes, it is.

Cate No. You. Doing that.

Ian When are you going to grow up?

Cate I don't believe in killing.

Ian You'll learn.

Cate No I won't.

Ian Can't always be taking it backing down letting them think they've got a right turn the other cheek SHIT

some things are worth more than that have to be
protected from shite.

Cate   I used to love you.

Ian   What's changed?

Cate   You.

Ian   No. Now you see me. That's all.

Cate   You're a nightmare.

She shakes.
Ian *watches a while, then hugs her.*
She is still shaking so he hugs tightly to stop her.

Cate   That hurts.

Ian   Sorry.

He hugs her less tightly.
He has a coughing fit.
He spits into his handkerchief and waits for the pain to subside.
Then he lights a cigarette.

Ian   How you feeling?

Cate   I ache.

Ian   *(Nods.)*

Cate   Everywhere.
I stink of you.

Ian   You want a bath?

Cate *begins to cough and retch.*
She puts her fingers down her throat and produces a hair.
She holds it up and looks at **Ian** *in disgust. She spits.*
Ian *goes into the bathroom and turns on one of the bath taps.*
Cate *stares out of the window.*
Ian *returns.*

Cate   Looks like there's a war on.

Ian   (*Doesn't look.*)

Turning into Wogland.
You coming to Leeds again?

Cate   Twenty-sixth.

Ian   Will you come and see me?

Cate   I'm going to the football.

She goes to the bathroom.
Ian *picks up the phone.*

Ian   Two English breakfasts, son.

He finishes the remainder of the gin.
Cate *returns.*

Cate   I can't piss. It's just blood.

Ian   Drink lots of water.

Cate   Or shit. It hurts.

Ian   It'll heal.

There is a knock at the door. They both jump.

Cate   DON'T ANSWER IT DON'T ANSWER IT
DON'T ANSWER IT

She dives on the bed and puts her head under the pillow.

Ian   Cate, shut up.

He pulls the pillow off and puts the gun to her head.

Cate   Do it. Go on, shoot me. Can't be no worse than what
you've done already. Shoot me if you want, then turn
it on yourself and do the world a favour.

Ian   (*Stares at her.*)

Cate   I'm not scared of you, Ian. Go on.

Ian   (*Gets off her.*)

Cate   (*Laughs.*)

Ian Answer the door and suck the cunt's cock.

> **Cate** *tries to open the door. It is locked.*
> **Ian** *throws the key at her.*
> *She opens the door.*
> *The breakfasts are outside on a tray. She brings them in.*
> **Ian** *locks the door.*
> **Cate** *stares at the food.*

Cate Sausages. Bacon.

Ian Sorry. Forgot. Swap your meat for my tomatoes and mushrooms. And toast.

Cate (*Begins to retch.*)

> The smell.

> **Ian** *takes a sausage off the plate and stuffs it in his mouth and keeps a rasher of bacon in his hand.*
> *He puts the tray of food under the bed with a towel over it.*

Ian Will you stay another day?

Cate I'm having a bath and going home.

> *She picks up her bag and goes into the bathroom, closing the door.*
> *We hear the other bath tap being turned on.*
> *There are two loud knocks at the outer door.*
> **Ian** *draws his gun, goes to the door and listens.*
> *The door is tried from outside. It is locked.*
> *There are two more loud knocks.*

Ian Who's there?

> *Silence.*
> *Then two more loud knocks.*

Ian Who's there?

> *Silence.*
> *Then two more knocks.*
> **Ian** *looks at the door.*
> *Then he knocks twice.*
> *Silence.*

Then two more knocks from outside.

Ian *thinks.*
Then he knocks three times.

Silence.
Three knocks from outside.

Ian *knocks once.*
One knock from outside.

Ian *knocks twice.*
Two knocks.

Ian *puts his gun back in the holster and unlocks the door.*

Ian   (*Under his breath.*) Speak the Queen's English fucking
nigger.

He opens the door.
Outside is a **Soldier** *with a sniper's rifle.*
Ian *tries to push the door shut and draw his revolver.*
The **Soldier** *pushes the door open and takes* **Ian**'s *gun*
easily.
The two stand, both surprised, staring at each other.
Eventually.

Soldier   What's that?

Ian *looks down and realises he is still holding a rasher of bacon.*

Ian   Pig.

The **Soldier** *holds out his hand.*
Ian *gives him the bacon and he eats it quickly, rind and all.*
The **Soldier** *wipes his mouth.*

Soldier   Got any more?

Ian   No.

Soldier   Got any more?

Ian   I –
No.

Soldier   Got any more?

Ian   (*Points to the tray under the bed.*)

> The **Soldier** *bends down carefully, never taking his eyes or rifle off* **Ian**, *and takes the tray from under the bed.*
> *He straightens up and glances down at the food.*

Soldier   Two.

Ian   I was hungry.

Soldier   I bet.

> The **Soldier** *sits on the edge of the bed and very quickly devours both breakfasts.*
> *He sighs with relief and burps.*
> *He nods towards the bathroom.*

Soldier   She in there?

Ian   Who?

Soldier   I can smell the sex.

> (*He begins to search the room.*)

> You a journalist?

Ian   I –

Soldier   Passport.

Ian   What for?

Soldier   (*Looks at him.*)

Ian   In the jacket.

> The **Soldier** *is searching a chest of drawers.*
> *He finds a pair of* **Cate**'s *knickers and holds them up.*

Soldier   Hers?

Ian   (*Doesn't answer.*)

Soldier   Or yours.

> (*He closes his eyes and rubs them gently over his face, smelling with pleasure.*)

What's she like?

Ian (*Doesn't answer.*)

Soldier Is she soft?
Is she – ?

Ian (*Doesn't answer.*)

> *The* **Soldier** *puts* **Cate**'s *knickers in his pocket and goes to the bathroom.*
> *He knocks on the door. No answer.*
> *He tries the door. It is locked.*
> *He forces it and goes in.*
> **Ian** *waits, in a panic.*
> *We hear the bath taps being turned off.*
> **Ian** *looks out of the window.*

Ian Jesus Lord.

> *The* **Soldier** *returns.*

Soldier Gone. Taking a risk. Lot of bastard soldiers out there.

> **Ian** *looks in the bathroom.* **Cate** *isn't there.*
> *The* **Soldier** *looks in* **Ian**'s *jacket pockets and takes his keys, wallet and passport.*

Soldier (*Looks at* **Ian**'s *press card.*)

Ian Jones.
Journalist.

Ian Oi.

Soldier Oi.

> *They stare at each other.*

Ian If you've come to shoot me –

Soldier (*Reaches out to touch* **Ian**'s *face but stops short of physical contact.*)

Ian   You taking the piss?

Soldier   Me?

(*He smiles.*)

Our town now.

(*He stands on the bed and urinates over the pillows.*)

Ian *is disgusted.*

There is a blinding light, then a huge explosion.

Blackout.

The sound of summer rain.

Scene Three

The hotel has been blasted by a mortar bomb.

There is a large hole in one of the walls, and everything is covered in dust which is still falling.

The **Soldier** *is unconscious, rifle still in hand.*
He has dropped **Ian***'s gun which lies between them.*

Ian *lies very still, eyes open.*

Ian   Mum?

Silence.
The **Soldier** *wakes and turns his eyes and rifle on* **Ian** *with the minimum possible movement.*
He instinctively runs his free hand over his limbs and body to check that he is still in one piece. He is.

Soldier   The drink.

Ian *looks around. There is a bottle of gin lying next to him with the lid off.*
He holds it up to the light.

Ian   Empty.

Soldier   (*Takes the bottle and drinks the last mouthful.*)

Ian   (*Chuckles.*)

>   Worse than me.

>   *The **Soldier** holds the bottle up and shakes it over his mouth, catching any remaining drops.*

>   **Ian** *finds his cigarettes in his shirt pocket and lights up.*

Soldier   Give us a cig.

Ian   Why?

Soldier   'Cause I've got a gun and you haven't.

>   **Ian** *considers the logic.*
>   *Then takes a single cigarette out of the packet and tosses it at the* **Soldier**.
>   *The **Soldier** picks up the cigarette and puts it in his mouth.*
>   *He looks at **Ian**, waiting for a light.*
>   **Ian** *holds out his cigarette.*
>   *The **Soldier** leans forward, touching the tip of his cigarette against the lit one, eyes always on **Ian**.*
>   *He smokes.*

Soldier   Never met an Englishman with a gun before, most of them don't know what a gun is. You a soldier?

Ian   Of sorts.

Soldier   Which side, if you can remember.

Ian   Don't know what the sides are here.
Don't know where . . .

>   (*He trails off confused, and looks at the **Soldier**.*)

>   Think I might be drunk.

Soldier   No. It's real.

>   (*He picks up the revolver and examines it.*)

>   Come to fight for us?

Ian   No, I –

Soldier   No, course not. English.

Ian   I'm Welsh.

Soldier   Sound English, fucking accent.

Ian   I live there.

Soldier   Foreigner?

Ian   English and Welsh is the same. British. I'm not an import.

Soldier   What's fucking Welsh, never heard of it.

Ian   Come over from God knows where have their kids and call them English they're not English born in England don't make you English.

Soldier   Welsh as in Wales?

Ian   It's attitude.

(*He turns away.*)

Look at the state of my fucking jacket. The bitch.

Soldier   Your girlfriend did that, angry was she?

Ian   She's not my girlfriend.

Soldier   What, then?

Ian   Mind your fucking own.

Soldier   Haven't been here long have you.

Ian   So?

Soldier   Learn some manners, Ian.

Ian   Don't call me that.

Soldier   What shall I call you?

Ian   Nothing.

Silence.

The **Soldier** *looks at* **Ian** *for a very long time, saying nothing.*
Ian *is uncomfortable.*
Eventually.

Ian   What?

Soldier   Nothing.

Silence.
Ian *is uneasy again.*

Ian   My name's Ian.

Soldier   I
Am
Dying to make love
Ian

Ian   (*Looks at him.*)

Soldier   You got a girlfriend?

Ian   (*Doesn't answer.*)

Soldier   I have.
Col.
Fucking beautiful.

Ian   Cate –

Soldier   Close my eyes and think about her.
She's –
She's –
She's –
She's –
She's –
She's –
She's –
When was the last time you – ?

Ian   (*Looks at him.*)

Soldier   When? I know it was recent, smell it, remember.

Ian   Last night. I think.

Soldier   Good?

Ian   Don't know. I was pissed. Probably not.

Soldier   Three of us –

Ian   Don't tell me.

Soldier   Went to a house just outside town. All gone. Apart
from a small boy hiding in the corner. One of the
others took him outside. Lay him on the ground
and shot him through the legs. Heard crying in the
basement. Went down. Three men and four
women. Called the others. They held the men while
I fucked the women. Youngest was twelve. Didn't
cry, just lay there. Turned her over and –
Then she cried. Made her lick me clean. Closed my
eyes and thought of –
Shot her father in the mouth. Brothers shouted.
Hung them from the ceiling by their testicles.

Ian   Charming.

Soldier   Never done that?

Ian   No.

Soldier   Sure?

Ian   I wouldn't forget.

Soldier   You would.

Ian   Couldn't sleep with myself.

Soldier   What about your wife?

Ian   I'm divorced.

Soldier   Didn't you ever –

Ian   No.

Soldier   What about that girl locked herself in the bathroom.

Ian   (*Doesn't answer.*)

Soldier   Ah.

Ian   You did four in one go, I've only ever done one.

Soldier   You killed her?

Ian   (*Makes a move for his gun.*)

Soldier   Don't, I'll have to shoot you. Then I'd be lonely.

Ian   Course I haven't.

Soldier   Why not, don't seem to like her very much.

Ian   I do.
She's . . . a woman.

Soldier   So?

Ian   I've never –
It's not –

Soldier   What?

Ian   (*Doesn't answer.*)

Soldier   Thought you were a soldier.

Ian   Not like that.

Soldier   Not like that, they're all like that.

Ian   My job –

Soldier   Even me. Have to be.
My girl –
Not going back to her. When I go back.
She's dead, see. Fucking bastard soldier, he –

He stops.
Silence.

Ian   I'm sorry.

Soldier   Why?

Ian   It's terrible.

Soldier   What is?

Ian   Losing someone, a woman, like that.

Soldier   You know, do you?

Ian   I –

Soldier   Like what?

Ian   Like –
You said –
A soldier –

Soldier   You're a soldier.

Ian   I haven't –

Soldier   What if you were ordered to?

Ian   Can't imagine it.

Soldier   Imagine it.

Ian   (*Imagines it.*)

Soldier   In the line of duty.
For your country.
Wales.

Ian   (*Imagines harder.*)

Soldier   Foreign slag.

Ian   (*Imagines harder. Looks sick.*)

Soldier   Would you?

Ian   (*Nods.*)

Soldier   How.

Ian   Quickly. Back of the head. Bam.

Soldier   That's all.

Ian   It's enough.

Soldier   You think?

Ian   Yes.

Soldier   You never killed anyone.

Ian   Fucking have.

Soldier   No.

Ian   Don't you fucking –

Soldier   Couldn't talk like this. You'd know.

Ian   Know what?

Soldier   Exactly. You don't know.

Ian   Know fucking what?

Soldier   Stay in the dark.

Ian   What? Fucking what? What don't I know?

Soldier   You think –

>   (*He stops and smiles.*)

>   I broke a woman's neck. Stabbed up between her legs, on the fifth stab snapped her spine.

Ian   (*Looks sick.*)

Soldier   You couldn't do that.

Ian   No.

Soldier   You never killed.

Ian   Not like that.

Soldier   Not
Like
That

Ian   I'm not a torturer.

Soldier   You're close to them, gun to head. Tie them up, tell them what you're going to do to them, make them wait for it, then . . . what?

Ian   Shoot them.

Soldier You haven't got a clue.

Ian What then?

Soldier You never fucked a man before you killed him?

Ian No.

Soldier Or after?

Ian Course not.

Soldier Why not?

Ian What for, I'm not queer.

Soldier Col, they buggered her. Cut her throat. Hacked her ears and nose off, nailed them to the front door.

Ian Enough.

Soldier Ever seen anything like that?

Ian Stop.

Soldier Not in photos?

Ian Never.

Soldier Some journalist, that's your job.

Ian What?

Soldier Proving it happened. I'm here, got no choice. But you. You should be telling people.

Ian No one's interested.

Soldier You can do something, for me –

Ian No.

Soldier Course you can.

Ian I can't do anything.

Soldier Try.

Ian   I write . . . stories. That's all. Stories. This isn't a story anyone wants to hear.

Soldier   Why not?

Ian   (*Takes one of the newspapers from the bed and reads.*)

'Kinky car dealer Richard Morris drove two teenage prostitutes into the country, tied them naked to fences and whipped them with a belt before having sex. Morris, from Sheffield, was jailed for three years for unlawful sexual intercourse with one of the girls, aged thirteen.'

(*He tosses the paper away.*)

Stories.

Soldier   Doing to them what they done to us, what good is that? At home I'm clean. Like it never happened. Tell them you saw me.
Tell them . . . you saw me.

Ian   It's not my job.

Soldier   Whose is it?

Ian   I'm a home journalist, for Yorkshire. I don't cover foreign affairs.

Soldier   Foreign affairs, what you doing here?

Ian   I do other stuff. Shootings and rapes and kids getting fiddled by queer priests and schoolteachers. Not soldiers screwing each other for a patch of land. It has to be . . . personal. Your girlfriend, she's a story. Soft and clean. Not you. Filthy, like the wogs. No joy in a story about blacks who gives a shit? Why bring you to light?

Soldier   You don't know fuck all about me.
I went to school.
I made love with Col.

Bastards killed her, now I'm here.
Now I'm here.

(*He pushes the rifle in* **Ian***'s face.*)

Turn over, Ian.

Ian Why?

Soldier Going to fuck you.

Ian No.

Soldier Kill you then.

Ian Fine.

Soldier See. Rather be shot than fucked and shot.

Ian Yes.

Soldier And now you agree with anything I say.

He kisses **Ian** *very tenderly on the lips.*
They stare at each other.

Soldier You smell like her. Same cigarettes.

The **Soldier** *turns* **Ian** *over with one hand.*
He holds the revolver to **Ian***'s head with the other.*
He pulls down **Ian***'s trousers, undoes his own and rapes him – eyes*
closed and smelling **Ian***'s hair.*
The **Soldier** *is crying his heart out.*

Ian*'s face registers pain but he is silent.*

When the **Soldier** *has finished he pulls up his trousers and pushes the*
revolver up **Ian***'s anus.*

Soldier Bastard pulled the trigger on Col.
What's it like?

Ian (*Tries to answer. He can't.*)

Soldier (*Withdraws the gun and sits next to* **Ian**.)

You never fucked by a man before?

Ian (*Doesn't answer.*)

Soldier Didn't think so. It's nothing. Saw thousands of people packing into trucks like pigs trying to leave town. Women threw their babies on board hoping someone would look after them. Crushing each other to death. Insides of people's heads came out of their eyes. Saw a child most of his face blown off, young girl I fucked hand up inside her trying to claw my liquid out, starving man eating his dead wife's leg. Gun was born here and won't die. Can't get tragic about your arse. Don't think your Welsh arse is different to any other arse I fucked. Sure you haven't got any more food, I'm fucking starving.

Ian Are you going to kill me?

Soldier Always covering your own arse.

The **Soldier** *grips* **Ian***'s head in his hands.*

He puts his mouth over one of **Ian***'s eyes, sucks it out, bites it off and eats it.*

He does the same to the other eye.

Soldier He ate her eyes.
Poor bastard.
Poor love.
Poor fucking bastard.

Blackout.

The sound of autumn rain.

Scene Four

The same.

The **Soldier** *lies close to* **Ian***, the revolver in his hand.*
He has blown his own brain out.

Cate *enters through the bathroom door, soaking wet and carrying a baby.*
She steps over the **Soldier** *with a glance.*
Then she sees **Ian**.

Cate   You're a nightmare.

Ian   Cate?

Cate   It won't stop.

Ian   Catie? You here?

Cate   Everyone in town is crying.

Ian   Touch me.

Cate   Soldiers have taken over.

Ian   They've won?

Cate   Most people gave up.

Ian   You seen Matthew?

Cate   No.

Ian   Will you tell him for me?

Cate   He isn't here.

Ian   Tell him –
Tell him –

Cate   No.

Ian   Don't know what to tell him.
I'm cold.
Tell him –
You here?

Cate   A woman gave me her baby.

Ian   You come for me, Catie? Punish me or rescue me makes no difference I love you Cate tell him for me do it for me touch me Cate.

Cate   Don't know what to do with it.

Ian   I'm cold.

Cate   Keeps crying.

Ian   Tell him –

Cate   I CAN'T.

Ian   Will you stay with me, Cate?

Cate   No.

Ian   Why not?

Cate   I have to go back soon.

Ian   Shaun know what we did?

Cate   No.

Ian   Better tell him.

Cate   No.

Ian   He'll know. Even if you don't.

Cate   How?

Ian   Smell it. Soiled goods. Don't want it, not when you can have someone clean.

Cate   What's happened to your eyes?

Ian   I need you to stay, Cate. Won't be for long.

Cate   Do you know about babies?

Ian   No.

Cate   What about Matthew?

Ian   He's twenty-four.

Cate   When he was born.

Ian   They shit and cry. Hopeless.

Cate   Bleeding.

Ian   Will you touch me?

Cate   No.

Ian   So I know you're here.

Cate   You can hear me.

Ian   Won't hurt you, I promise.

Cate   (*Goes to him slowly and touches the top of his head.*)

Ian   Help me.

Cate   (*Strokes his hair.*)

Ian   Be dead soon anyway, Cate.
And it hurts.
Help me to –
Help me –
Finish
It

Cate   (*Withdraws her hand.*)

Ian   Catie?

Cate   Got to get something for Baby to eat.

Ian   Won't find anything.

Cate   May as well look.

Ian   Fucking bastards ate it all.

Cate   It'll die.

Ian   Needs its mother's milk.

Cate   Ian.

Ian   Stay.
Nowhere to go, where are you going to go?
Bloody dangerous on your own, look at me.
Safer here with me.

Cate *considers.*
Then sits down with the baby some distance from **Ian**.
He relaxes when he hears her sit.

Cate *rocks the baby.*

Ian Not as bad as all that, am I?

Cate (*Looks at him.*)

Ian Will you help me, Catie?

Cate How.

Ian Find my gun?

Cate *thinks.*
Then gets up and searches around, baby in arms.
She sees the revolver in the **Soldier**'s *hand and stares at it for some*
time.

Ian Found it?

Cate No.

She takes the revolver from the **Soldier** *and fiddles with it.*
It springs open and she stares in at the bullets.
She removes them and closes the gun.

Ian That it?

Cate Yes.

Ian Can I have it?

Cate I don't think so.

Ian Catie.

Cate What?

Ian Come on.

Cate Don't tell me what to do.

Ian I'm not, love. Can you keep that baby quiet.

Cate It's not doing anything. It's hungry.

Ian We're all bloody hungry, don't shoot myself I'll starve to
death.

Cate It's wrong to kill yourself.

Ian   No it's not.

Cate   God wouldn't like it.

Ian   There isn't one.

Cate   How do you know?

Ian   No God. No Father Christmas. No fairies. No Narnia. No fucking nothing.

Cate   Got to be something.

Ian   Why?

Cate   Doesn't make sense otherwise.

Ian   Don't be fucking stupid, doesn't make sense anyway. No reason for there to be a God just because it would be better if there was.

Cate   Thought you didn't want to die.

Ian   I can't see.

Cate   My brother's got blind friends. You can't give up.

Ian   Why not?

Cate   It's weak.

Ian   I know you want to punish me, trying to make me live.

Cate   I don't.

Ian   Course you fucking do, I would. There's people I'd love to suffer but they don't, they die and that's it.

Cate   What if you're wrong?

Ian   I'm not.

Cate   But if.

Ian   I've seen dead people. They're dead. They're not somewhere else, they're dead.

Cate   What about people who've seen ghosts?

Ian   What about them? Imagining it. Or making it up or wishing the person was still alive.

Cate   People who've died and come back say they've seen tunnels and lights –

Ian   Can't die and come back. That's not dying, it's fainting. When you die, it's the end.

Cate   I believe in God.

Ian   Everything's got a scientific explanation.

Cate   No.

Ian   Give me my gun.

Cate   What are you going to do?

Ian   I won't hurt you.

Cate   I know.

Ian   End it.
Got to, Cate, I'm ill.
Just speeding it up a bit.

Cate   (*Thinks hard.*)

Ian   Please.

Cate   (*Gives him the gun.*)

Ian   (*Takes the gun and puts it in his mouth.
He takes it out again.*)

Don't stand behind me.

*He puts the gun back in his mouth.
He pulls the trigger. The gun clicks, empty.
He shoots again. And again and again and again.
He takes the gun out of his mouth.*

Ian   Fuck.

Cate   Fate, see. You're not meant to do it. God –

Ian   The cunt.

(*He throws the gun away in despair.*)

Cate   (*Rocks the baby and looks down at it.*)

Oh no.

Ian   What.

Cate   It's dead.

Ian   Lucky bastard.

Cate   (*Bursts out laughing, unnaturally, hysterically, uncontrollably. She laughs and laughs and laughs and laughs and laughs.*)

Blackout.

The sound of heavy winter rain.

Scene Five

The same.

Cate *is burying the baby under the floor.*

She looks around and finds two pieces of wood.
*She rips the lining out of **Ian**'s jacket and binds the wood together in a cross which she sticks into the floor.*
She collects a few of the scattered flowers and places them under the cross.

Cate   I don't know her name.

Ian   Don't matter. No one's going to visit.

Cate   I was supposed to look after her.

Ian   Can bury me next to her soon. Dance on my grave.

Cate   Don't feel no pain or know nothing you shouldn't know –

Ian   Cate?

Cate   Shh.

Ian   What you doing?

Cate   Praying. Just in case.

Ian   Will you pray for me?

Cate   No.

Ian   When I'm dead, not now.

Cate   No point when you're dead.

Ian   You're praying for her.

Cate   She's baby.

Ian   So?

Cate   Innocent.

Ian   Can't you forgive me?

Cate   Don't see bad things or go bad places –

Ian   She's dead, Cate.

Cate   Or meet anyone who'll do bad things.

Ian   She won't, Cate, she's dead.

Cate   Amen.

   (*She starts to leave.*)

Ian   Where you going?

Cate   I'm hungry.

Ian   Cate, it's dangerous. There's no food.

Cate   Can get some off a soldier.

Ian   How?

Cate   (*Doesn't answer.*)

Ian   Don't do that.

Cate   Why not?

Ian That's not you.

Cate I'm hungry.

Ian I know so am I.
But.
I'd rather –
It's not –
Please, Cate.
I'm blind.

Cate I'm hungry.

(She goes.)

Ian Cate? Catie?
If you get some food –
Fuck.

Darkness.
Light.

Ian *masturbating.*

Ian cunt cunt cunt cunt cunt cunt cunt cunt cunt cunt cunt

Darkness.
Light.

Ian *strangling himself with his bare hands.*

Darkness.
Light.

Ian *shitting.*
And then trying to clean it up with newspaper.

Darkness.
Light.

Ian *laughing hysterically.*

Darkness.
Light.

Ian *having a nightmare.*

Darkness.
Light.

Ian *crying, huge bloody tears.*
He is hugging the **Soldier***'s body for comfort.*

Darkness.
Light.

Ian *lying very still, weak with hunger.*

Darkness.
Light.

Ian *tears the cross out of the ground, rips up the floor and lifts the baby's body out.*

He eats the baby.

He puts the remains back in the baby's blanket and puts the bundle back in the hole.
A beat, then he climbs in after it and lies down, head poking out of the floor.

He dies with relief.

It starts to rain on him, coming through the roof.

Eventually.

Ian   Shit.

Cate *enters carrying some bread, a large sausage and a bottle of gin. There is blood seeping from between her legs.*

Cate   You're sitting under a hole.

Ian   I know.

Cate   Get wet.

Ian   Aye.

Cate   Stupid bastard.

She pulls a sheet off the bed and wraps it around her.

She sits next to **Ian**'s *head.*

She eats her fill of the sausage and bread, then washes it down with gin.

Ian *listens.*

She feeds **Ian** *with the remaining food.*

She pours gin in **Ian**'s *mouth.*

She finishes feeding **Ian** *and sits apart from him, huddled for warmth.*

She drinks the gin.
She sucks her thumb.

Silence.

It rains.

Ian   Thank you.

Blackout.

Commentary

Blasted is not the kind of play that leaves one feeling apathetic. For those familiar with Sarah Kane's work or who at least know of her reputation as a writer of confrontational theatre, it might be easy to forget how shocking this play is to the first-time reader or audience member. I imagine those who just read the play for the first time probably experienced moments of disgust, horror, sadness and even laughter. Yet once those initial emotions subside, the play leaves us with a myriad of questions:

> What inspired Kane to write this play?
> Why is Ian (to be blunt) such a bastard?
> What causes Cate to have those fits?
> Where does the Soldier come from?
> What happens to the hotel when the bomb explodes?
> Is what happens to Ian and Cate real or is it a dream?
> What does the end of the play mean?
> How do you stage this seemingly impossible play?

Fear not, first-timers, you are not alone in asking such questions, for even veterans of Kane's work are still grappling with them and this commentary will not, I'm afraid, offer definitive answers. That would be an impossible and foolhardy task. *Blasted* invites multiple interpretations; its aim is to put the audience through an experience rather than put forward a conclusive argument. This commentary will explore potential avenues for understanding the play. Before grappling with the play's content, it is helpful to put *Blasted* in a historical and theatrical context, for this was not a play that appeared quietly on the British stage, and its arresting use of form has antecedents in the history of modern drama.

'This disgusting feast of filth'

The first production of *Blasted* is now the stuff of legend.
Though now firmly part of the canon of important British
plays, *Blasted* was at first the subject of great controversy and
the furore reached such intensity that some suggested the
theatre that premiered the play should have its funding taken
away as punishment for programming it. The first play by the
then-unknown writer opened on 12 January 1995 at the Royal
Court Theatre's smaller Upstairs space. January is typically a
quiet month for London theatre, following the long Christmas
holiday and before the major spring openings. Kane suspected
that a few people at the Royal Court were, in her words,
'embarrassed' by the play, and 'put it into a spot after Christmas
when no one was going to the theatre.'[1] Typically at the
Theatre Upstairs, the press nights were spread over two
performances, but because of another opening (of Strindberg's
The Dance of Death at the Almeida Theatre) that same week,
the majority of critics came to see the show on the same night,
and on the evening of 18 January critics and their guests
occupied forty-five of the sixty-two seats in the small Theatre
Upstairs – a tough crowd by anyone's standards.

Even though only one reviewer walked out of the show, the
critics smelled a story. Here was a play littered with startling
atrocities, and which used a theatrical vocabulary hostile to the
demands of naturalism. A show that began as a quintessential
Royal Court play, worthy of John Obsorne at his most
misanthropic, but updated for the 1990s, suddenly became
something surreal. An unnamed soldier rapes and mutilates a
journalist called Ian in a Leeds hotel room that is transformed
in the middle of the play into a battlefield, one which, at
that time, conjured up the atrocities occurring in Bosnia.
Furthermore, this was a play by a woman. The largely male
critics were not pleased with a play that diverged so far from
what was perceived to be the issue-based women's theatre of
Sarah Daniels and Timberlake Wertenbaker. How could such
things, these critics asked, be allowed to occur on the Royal
Court's stage?

The next morning, the headline of the *Daily Mail*'s review said it all: 'This disgusting feast of filth'. The first line of Jack Tinker's review is the stuff of a playwright's dreams and nightmares: 'Until last night I thought I was immune from shock in any theatre. I am not.'[2] Charles Spencer of the *Daily Telegraph* felt Tinker's pain: 'Hardened theatre critics looked in danger of parting company with their suppers.'[3] The result of such 'bad' press? The play's short three-week run immediately sold out, overnight Sarah Kane became a *cause célèbre*, and *Blasted* became the most talked about, least seen play of the decade in her home country.

The critics' comments about Kane's writing showed a complete lack of understanding about the play's subversion of the naturalistic form. Such attacks could not but sting the young playwright. After listing every violent and sexual act in the play, the *Guardian*'s Michael Billington wondered 'how such naive tosh managed to scrape past the Royal Court's normally judicious play-selection committee'.[4] The condemnation of Kane's writing remains startlingly cruel: 'She isn't a good writer' (*Daily Telegraph*); 'Utterly without dramatic merit' (*Daily Mail*); 'Lacks even the logic of a dream' (*Independent on Sunday*); 'A truly terrible little play' (*International Herald Tribune*).

Only months before, theatre critics had been bemoaning the dearth of exciting new writing for the stage. Billington, for instance, in November 1994 deemed the London stage 'a dusty museum rather than [the] turbulent forum' it once had been.[5] Two years earlier, Benedict Nightingale of *The Times* ironically called the revival of J.B. Priestley's 1946 play *An Inspector Calls* the 'most contemporary play in London' that year.[6] When Kane's play was first staged, there was a general sense that British playwriting was on the decline. Billington concluded in 1991 that 'new drama no longer occupies the central position it has in British theatre over the past thirty-five years', and he criticised new writing for its 'small scale nature', which 'increasingly privatises experience'.[7] In a joint letter to the *Guardian* in 1994, eighty-seven playwrights decried the significant drop in productions of new plays. David Edgar drolly noted that in the years following 1988, 'there were major outbreaks of *Seagulls*, *Blithe Spirits* [and] *Doll's Houses*'.[8] This plague of revivals, Edgar argued, was at the expense of new *Caretakers*, *Loots* and *Look Back in Angers*. Instead of a playwrights' theatre, the British stage had become a market for directors like Deborah Warner and Tim Supple, who were reinventing the classics or adapting novels for the stage.

Yet when Kane's original voice emerged, the critics clearly did not know what to make of the play and instead of grappling with the material, they opted for indignation, real or otherwise. The discourse about Kane and her play deteriorated to the point that a headline read, 'Rape Play Girl Goes into Hiding' (*Daily Express*), though in truth, Kane attended nearly every performance of her play. Such dismissals were not to last. By 2001, Billington, perhaps influenced by Harold Pinter's admiration for it, revised his initial assessment of *Blasted*; though still finding the play 'flawed', he now called it 'a humane, impassioned dramatic testament'.[9] It is a sentiment that he restated in his review of the 2010 revival at the Lyric, Hammersmith: 'Maybe [*Blasted* is] not a great play but it bears the stigmata of talent.'[10]

The maelstrom that greeted *Blasted*'s first production may have made it appear as if the critics and audiences were unanimous in their disapproval, but Kane's work had its vocal supporters. The *Mail on Sunday* review compared Kane to Strindberg and called the play's dialogue 'sparse and stunning'. Theatre luminaries including Edward Bond, David Edgar, Caryl Churchill and Harold Pinter, along with younger playwright David Greig and the Bush's literary manager Nick Drake, wrote to papers such as the *Guardian* in support of the play. The *Observer* even published a postscript to the *Blasted* controversy, appearing the day after the production closed. After comparing Kane's play to Shakespeare and Seneca, its final sentence read, 'I can hardly wait to see what Ms Kane does next.'[11] The *Observer* critic was not alone in feeling excitement about what was coming, for the doldrums that plagued the British stage were soon to be replaced by what some critics would call a 'renaissance' in playwriting.

Blasted and new writing in the 1990s

In the years that followed its first production, *Blasted* came to be regarded as one of the key plays written by a new generation of British playwrights called by a variety of names: 'in-yer-face', the 'New Brutalists', the 'theatre of urban ennui', or, less flatteringly, the 'blood-and-sperm generation'. Writers such as Kane, Mark Ravenhill, Martin McDonagh, Anthony Neilson and Joe Penhall were lumped together, despite significant differences in their writing, but their age and interest in violence and sex invited such connections. *Blasted*, for better or worse, made Kane 'in-yer-face'. Kane, however, is ultimately an individual voice, not truly part of any movement. Yet looking at plays by Kane and the other significant playwrights of the period (Ravenhill, McDonagh, David Greig, Jez Butterworth, Patrick Marber and others) does reveal a developing fault line in British theatre.

New writing was re-establishing its central place and the theatre was once again becoming the 'turbulent forum' that Billington desired. The younger playwrights challenged established writers such as David Hare, David Edgar and Howard Brenton. Kane was an astute student of the theatre and while she appreciated the work of the older generation, her plays and the work of her peers broke with the tradition of critical realism that had been the dominant style of British play-writing. Critical realism can be understood as verisimilitude with a clear point of view, realism with a thesis. This aesthetic had become the mainstay of the British stage since 1950s naturalism was married to 1960s political theatre during the 1970s and 1980s. By uniting Stanislavski and Brecht, critical realism aimed not only to reflect reality, but to take a critical stance in relation to that reality, in order, presumably, for an audience to imagine how it could be altered. This style is evident in the plays of Brenton, Hare and Edgar, even in the early plays of Caryl Churchill and Howard Barker, and it was popularised in productions by directors like Max Stafford-Clark and William Gaskill, whose company Joint Stock created a lasting model for the development of plays out of research and workshops. The younger writers appeared to have a different style that rejected any pedagogical function for drama and to be highly interested in 'shocking' subject matter.

Many of the same critics who attacked *Blasted* changed their tune in the wake of the success of Mark Ravenhill's *Shopping and Fucking*, first staged (also at the Royal Court Theatre Upstairs) the year after *Blasted*. By the time the play – whose title couldn't even be printed on posters – enjoyed a lengthy West End run in 1997, talk of a new Golden Age abounded and critics were already discussing a possible 'movement'. Benedict Nightingale made comparisons between this new work and the Angry Young Men of the 1950s, and talked about a new kind of British play. Billington commented in 1996, 'I cannot recall a time when there were so many exciting dramatists in the twenty-something age group.'[12] Critic Aleks Sierz, then theatre critic for *Tribune*, quickly became the leading champion of this new brand of writing, through his articles and eventually the first book devoted to these writers published in 2001. In his numerous writings on the subject, Sierz branded these writers 'in-yer-face', a name that has proved to have staying power. He saw debacles over plays by Philip Ridley and Anthony Neilson during the early part of the 1990s as harbingers of a new sensibility of cruelty and shock. Though shock was not new to the British stage, that aesthetic, Sierz argues, became in the 1990s the dominant feature of new writing at theatres such as the Royal Court and the Bush.

Dubbing Kane 'in-yer-face' does a disservice to her since it pigeonholes her work as simply 'shocking'. Yet placing *Blasted* alongside the other popular and controversial plays of the period – works such as Ravenhill's *Shopping and Fucking*, Butterworth's *Mojo*, McDonagh's *The Beauty Queen of Leenane*, to name but three – does reveal a number of shared characteristics and aesthetic concerns. Rather than dubbing them a 'movement' of 'in-yer-face' writers, we can instead locate what philosopher Ludwig Wittgenstein calls 'family resemblances'. Wittgenstein argues for recognising connections between things based on a 'resemblance' that does not have to be reduced to a simple generality. He sees this as akin to how we recognise the 'various resemblances between family members: build, features, colour of eyes, gait, temperament, etc. etc.' Therefore, rather than finding an essential commonality between the work of these playwrights, we can instead locate 'a complicated network of similarities, overlapping and criss-crossing: sometimes overall similarities, sometimes similarities of detail'.[13] I find ten 'resemblances' in the new writing of this period, and these characteristics reveal how this work breaks from the concerns of previous generations:

1. The importance of shock in language and stage imagery, as part of a rejection of 'political correctness'.

2. The investment in cruelty as subject matter and as part of the audience's viewing experience.

3. An exploration of gender roles and sexual mores, seen most often in an obsession with fathers and father-figures, which is representative of the so-called 1990s 'Crisis of Masculinity'.

4. The move away from large political plays, the so-called 'State of the Nation [England]' plays, towards smaller-cast works that focus on individual struggles.

5. The rejection of characters who can be clearly distinguished as either victim or oppressor; victims can be complicit in their own oppression, while oppressors also suffer as victims.

6. The rejection of characters as 'spokespeople' for certain political ideologies or as 'stand-ins' for a moral authorial presence, a tendency found in the critical realist tradition of the 1970s and 1980s, where drama functions as a kind of journalism.

7. An uneasiness with labels such as 'minority' or 'feminist', in part as a way of separating the writers from the issue-based work of many 1980s writers and theatre companies.

8. In the wake of the collapse of Communism and the disintegration of Left and Right political oppositions, a general scepticism toward partisan politics of any stripe.

9. Some of these writers, including Kane, Ravenhill, Greig and Neilson, experimented with form and style, inspired by

European and American theatre, British mavericks such as
Howard Barker and Caryl Churchill, and the growing field
of 'live art'.

10. The acceptance of theatre's role as a commodity, marked
by an investment in 'coolness' and celebrity, with no
pretence of seeing theatre as outside of, or opposed to,
popular culture and mass media; seen most notably in the
appropriation of a pop-music sensibility.

This list gives a sense of the new theatre's concerns as well
as the ways in which it broke from previous British theatre
traditions. One main target for these writers was the work of
David Hare and his generation of playwrights who, by the
1990s, had become the prevailing standard for new British
writing. Critical realism, defined above, reached its apotheosis
with Hare's trilogy *Racing Demon* (1990), *Murmuring Judges*
(1991) and *The Absence of War* (1993). The entire trilogy was
staged at the National Theatre in October 1993 by Richard
Eyre, with each play focusing on a British institution – the
clergy, the legal system and the Labour Party. While many
critics perceived it to be a triumph of post-war drama ('a
stirring evening', Billington exclaimed), many younger theatre
artists saw Hare's trilogy as the complete absorption of 1970s
theatre into the establishment: Leftist art for limousine liberals,
written by a man who once extolled the virtues of Tory MP
John Major ('For the first time since I became an adult, I am
ruled by a man who appears fundamentally decent and honest')
and who attacked the 'sycophancy' of knighthoods in 1995
only to accept one himself three years later.[14]

There was also a desire to move beyond the ideas of the
feminist playwrights of the 1980s. The new playwrights, of
course, benefited from what writers as diverse as Margaretta
D'Arcy, Sarah Daniels, Pam Gems and Winsome Pinnock
accomplished, bringing issues of gender and race centre stage,
and in the process, opening doors for women theatre artists
during the dark days of Thatcher and Major. But labels such
as 'female playwright' and 'minority writer' were seen by the
new generation to be a straitjacket, limiting the potential for

creativity. Kane, in an interview published in 1997, raised a few eyebrows on this topic. When asked about her 'greatest responsibility' as a 'woman writer' by the interviewer, Kane responded:

> I have no responsibility as a woman writer because I don't believe there's such a thing. When people talk about me as a writer, that's what I am, and that's how I want my work to be judged – on its quality, not on the basis of my age, gender, class, sexuality, or race.[15]

Kane's detractors used statements such as these to attack her work as self-loathing or anti-feminist. But in truth, Kane was not alone in such sentiments. Many of the women playwrights who rose to prominence in the 1980s such as Timberlake Wertenbaker and Caryl Churchill felt similarly unsure about the labels being applied to them by the press.

In the 1990s, there was a widespread wariness about being pigeonholed by one's race, gender or sexual preference, since it was perceived as limiting the kinds of plays that you could write or the audiences that you could reach with your work. Ravenhill, for instance, set his work apart from more traditional gay-themed theatre by embracing the idea of the queer. The male characters of *Shopping and Fucking* have sex with other men, but it does not define them. The lead character Mark, for instance, has sexual appetites that do not discriminate based on gender; rent boys and Princess Diana were both fair game. The Soldier of Kane's *Blasted* rapes both men and women; to him, during war, the sex of the victim is superfluous, what matters is enacting retribution.

With writers like David Hare and Sarah Daniels nixed as possible role models, the names most often dropped by the 1990s playwrights come from an alternative tradition of British theatre: the plays and theoretical writings of Howard Barker; the influential canon of Samuel Beckett; the recent work of Caryl Churchill (who by the 1990s had moved far from the critical realism of Joint Stock into a surrealist style) and Martin Crimp (whose plays exhibit a decidedly continental flavour); the 'theatre of mixed means' or devised work which emphasised performance over written text (such as the work of Theatre de Complicite and Forced Entertainment).

Kane, in particular, looked to a European avant-garde for inspiration. In an interview with Nils Tabert, the German translator of her work, Kane said her influences were 'mainly non-English stuff', naming Antonin Artaud, Franz Kafka, Georges Bataille and Heiner Müller among others.[16] She also remarked elsewhere that reading Rainer Werner Fassbinder's play *Pre-Paradise Sorry Now* gave her the initial idea for *Crave*, her fourth play.[17] Closer to home, British director Jeremy Weller's *Mad* played an influential role in the development of her aesthetic. *Mad* was a devised piece by Weller's Grassmarket Project, and comprised a number of monologues and scenes concerning the theme of mental illness. Many of the performers in the piece were non-actors who suffered from the mental illnesses that they were describing, blurring the line between fiction and reality, and the play's structure was largely improvised, enhancing its documentary quality.

The experience of seeing *Mad* revealed to Kane the kind of theatre she wanted to make: 'It was a very unusual piece of theatre because it was totally experiential as opposed to speculatory. [. . .] *Mad* took me to hell, and the night I saw it I made a decision about the kind of theatre I wanted to make – experiential.'[18] So while the plays of Patrick Marber and Martin McDonagh, for instance, uphold traditional dramatic structure, Kane along with David Greig and Anthony Neilson moved British theatre further away from the critical realism that had been dominant in the previous two decades.

Politically, these writers are Thatcher's children. They came of age during a time when Thatcherite politics went largely unchallenged by a weakened Labour Party. They witnessed the eventual collapse of Socialism, which crushed the hopes of the Old Left. The steadfast rejection of labels ('woman writer', 'gay theatre') and the refusal to make characters political stand-ins or representative of simple binaries – good/bad, oppressed/oppressor, Left/Right – are evidence of a political uncertainty and a general scepticism about political content in art, or even politics at large. As a certain theatre joke goes, you could always tell who the good characters are in a David Hare play, because they are the ones wearing the jeans, not the suit (case in point: 1995's *Skylight*). That Leftist theatre could be reduced to a conflict between clothing choices attests to a deep ambivalence towards the idea of a play as a vehicle for a message.

Seen in this light, the importance that these writers place on moments of violent cruelty is not just a way to show the world 'as it is'; rather, at its best, shock serves as a means of challenging cynical complacency without necessarily falling back on any accepted paradigm for change, be it socialist, liberal or conservative. In a key way, the new writing of the 1990s shared the central desire of the historical avant-garde. The avant-garde's attack on the 'status of art' did not aim to make the content of art 'socially significant', but instead concerned itself with the work's effect, 'the way art functions in society'.[19] While Howard Brenton's *Weapons of Happiness* (1976) can end with factory workers living off the land and exploring the possibilities of Communism, or Sarah Daniels's *Neaptide* (1986) can close with an image of mother and daughter coming together to fight the forces of patriarchy, the drama of the 1990s cannot envision such idealistic conclusions in either art or life. Its young writers were keenly aware of how any radical political message in art could be absorbed by the marketplace and the powers-that-be for their own conservative ends.

The extreme acts on stage, therefore, were not a way of speaking to an audience, but a way to grab complacent theatregoers by their proverbial 'balls'. As Martin McDonagh succinctly put it, 'Why should anyone pay ten or twenty pounds to be lectured at for two hours?'[20] Getting an audience to feel was the order of the day, and this was not necessarily done at the expense of thinking, but certainly the visceral experiences of watching these plays often made reflection occur long after the curtain had fallen. Seeing a play such as *Blasted* in the confines of a small theatre like the Royal Court Upstairs or New York's Soho Rep (where the 2008 New York premiere was staged) increases the power of Kane's brutal imagery. I find watching a production of *Blasted* to be not solely about watching the narrative unfold on stage, but about the 'sensation' of that experience. This is theatre that desires to produce a physical effect on an audience. When watching the New York production directed by Sarah Benson, the couple sitting next to me literally couldn't watch the moment when Ian is raped; they put their heads in their laps. That 'Sensation' is also the name of one of the best-known exhibits of new British art in the 1990s hardly seems a coincidence.

The plays of the time are, then, obsessed with the perceived crisis in gender roles, specifically the so-called 'Crisis of Masculinity,' where the group that had once been the norm found its dominance threatened. Stories about the lack or failure of fathers recur with startling frequency in the plays of the 1990s – in, for instance, *Blasted*, *Shopping and Fucking* and *Mojo*. This interest in the figure of the father, more than just an age-old obsession dating back to the Greeks, can be understood politically, as a consequence of growing up under Thatcher. One can hypothesise that a leader who portrays all government assistance as 'paternalism' leads a generation to have a love-hate relationship with the male caregiver, seeing him as violent, inept or just not there when you need him. As a result, community becomes suspect and an individual must look out for himself or herself alone. We will return to the issue of masculinity in Kane's *Blasted* later in the commentary.

Finally, and perhaps most disturbing to those critics still sceptical of this new writing, these formal and political concerns often coexist with an unrivalled investment in coolness and celebrity. There is no pretence to see theatre as outside, or opposed to, popular culture and other forms of mass media. There is a clear appropriation of a pop-music sensibility in the way these writers are marketed by theatres, and in the way they market themselves to the press and their fans. Ravenhill, though perhaps only half-serious, said a great deal when he referred to *Shopping and Fucking* as a 'piece of Brit-pop'. These writers invoked pop music and film to demonstrate their kinship with cutting-edge popular culture, and to distance themselves from an art form that they feared appeared stodgy and out-of-date to their contemporaries. Anthony Neilson considers good theatre to be 'equivalent to punk rock'. 'It should be like going to see a good live band' was a sentiment with which Kane agreed, writing in the *Guardian* that she wished theatre could be more like the Jesus and Mary Chain gig that she saw during the final tour in 1998 of the indie band known for its earsplitting feedback and the Reid brothers' onstage fighting. Martin McDonagh cited both music and popular film as touchstones: 'I think people should leave theatre with the same feeling you get after a really good rock concert. My aim is to get as much [action film director] John Woo into the theatre as possible.' Kane one-upped the boys by listing football, the *real* 'drama with balls', as one of her favourite theatre experiences.[21]

If the playwright was becoming marginalised from what was most exciting about theatre in the early 1990s, such writers were now asserting their position at the centre of British theatre and worked hard to court their new-found celebrity. The controversy surrounding *Blasted* not only allowed critics to recognise retrospectively an emerging dominant strand in new writing, it also allowed the playwright to return to the prominent place that the Angry Young Men of the 1950s or the political playwrights of the 1970s enjoyed. But what was strikingly different about writers such as Ravenhill, McDonagh and Butterworth was how readily they embraced commodity culture and how easily commodity culture embraced their controversial work. Though they might have been wary of labels like 'in-yer-face' or 'New Brutalist', they were not afraid to brand themselves as 'cool'.

The idea of the 'cool' was at the forefront of popular discussion about British arts in the 1990s. The phenomenon known as 'Cool Britannia,' first popularised by the magazines *Newsweek* and *Time* in 1995 and 1996, hyped the revitalisation of British culture by rebranding London as the global capital of coolness, saying that 'Swinging London' was back. Robert Hewison, writing in 1998, sums up the dizzying excitement of 'Cool Britannia': 'From Brit-pop to Bryn Terfel, from Stephen Daldry to Damien Hirst, from Jenny Saville to Nicholas Hytner, from Rachel Whiteread to Mark Wigglesworth, there is a renewed sense of creative vigour and excitement.'[22] In Hewison's hit parade, high-profile stage directors such as Stephen Daldry and Nicholas Hytner stand beside rising art and music stars like Damien Hirst and Bryn Terfel. This line-up attests to the fact that theatre's contribution to this phenomenon was far from paltry. David Edgar called theatre the 'fifth leg of the new Swinging London', taking its place along side 'pop, fashion, fine art and food'.[23]

By rethinking the UK as a global exporter of culture, 'Cool Britannia' hoped to shake off the perception of England as a backward-looking island of stodgy tea parties and frumpy monarchs, and it sought to accomplish this feat by erasing the boundaries between high art and popular culture. In the words of one advertising executive, the art and fashion of the period was reimagined as 'a large advertising campaign on behalf of [England].'[24] What 'Cool Britannia' attempted to do was transform British popular culture and art into a brand that could market the country to the world at large. Tony Blair, the Prime Minister of Britain from 1997 to 2007, connected New Labour intimately with 'Cool Britannia' in order to gain popular support, especially from younger voters, and to disguise the more conservative aspects of 'New Labour'. Like most pop cultural phenomena, 'Cool Britannia' was short-lived: *Newsweek* rescinded its initial championing of all things British by issuing the headline 'Uncool Britannia' in June 1998. But the re-emergence of the playwright as a force on the British stage *and* the playwrights' own articulation of their position in culture sits nicely alongside the moment of 'Cool Britannia', even if fashion and music were typically seen as the prime exports of British culture to the globe.

These 'family resemblances' show the shared concerns of Kane's generation, but as any family dinner tends to remind us, members of the same family are far from clones of one another. It must also be emphasised how distinct Kane's voice was. Kane's generation of playwrights might have shed the critical or journalistic elements of the previous generation's work, but the majority of 1990s new writing remained largely realistic, while Kane's work shed verisimilitude with a vengeance. Her peers largely set their plays in specifically British or Irish contexts, while Kane strove for Beckettian universality. If McDonagh and Butterworth wrote with a kind of 'cool' detachment, Kane aimed for the opposite. In fact, the violence of her work, particularly in *Blasted*, is the opposite of 'cool'. In James Macdonald's or Sarah Benson's productions of the play, the violence makes you deeply uncomfortable, even sick to your stomach; it is never done as a joke or put in smart quotes. If McDonagh's heroes were film-makers like Quentin Tarantino or John Woo, Kane's were Beckett and Barker. In fact she critiqued Tarantino's films, finding them 'not about violence', but instead 'the representation of violence', and she cited Tarantino's use of music during a scene of torture in *Reservoir Dogs* as making violence more palatable to audiences.[25]

So while Kane's work might have emerged during the time of 'Cool Britannia', it can be read as a riposte or counter to the dominant idea of 'coolness' which is highly individualistic and detached.[26] Kane's plays – and this is part of their popularity – feel deeply personal, and even though they are works of fiction, they create a sense of connection between the writer and her audience; especially in her final play, *4.48 Psychosis*, it is as if she is sharing something heartfelt with us. What could be less 'cool' than that? While many of her peers had critical and commercial success, Kane's work did not reach large audiences in her own country until after her death in 1999; her third play, *Cleansed*, for instance, played to an average of fourteen per cent houses when it was first performed in 1998 on the Royal Court Theatre's main stage, then housed at the Duke of York's Theatre in the West End during the Sloane Square renovations. Her work had a small number of prominent productions in the first decade of the twenty-first century in the UK. Yet the plays are not revived in England with the frequency that they are staged on the continent. Kane's influence on newer writers remains unclear. Her experimentalism has not dominated new writing for the British stage, and the brutality of her work has even become the target of the occasional parody (Chris Lee's *Crushed*, for instance).

Despite these differences, the idea that Kane was the leader of a new generation of playwrights is too enticing for many critics. The *Blasted* premiere was reported in the press as a dramatic event of the highest order. There are the bad guys – Tinker and his fellow critics – who gang up on a female writer and her art, but the purveyors of good – the Royal Court, fellow playwrights and other critics – eventually outwit them, thus making sure both art and artist are 'redeemed'. The drama that surrounded *Blasted* overshadowed the play itself; the audiences of the first production could not see the play outside of the controversy. And this had an impact far beyond Kane's work.

The *Blasted* redemption narrative, the one that played itself out in the arts pages and on radio and TV programmes, was able to take distinct and random theatrical events that preceded the production as well as those that would follow, and transform them into a larger narrative: a new Golden Age, a renaissance of British playwriting. The 1995 production of *Blasted* was no longer a singular event, but part of a new trend, a new kind of play. Dots got connected; anomalies from earlier in the decade became harbingers, and future events now had a precursor to which to be compared. That ground zero was *Blasted* and not, say, Judy Upton's *Ashes and Sand*, the play which preceded Kane's at the Royal Court Upstairs, may have more to do with extenuating circumstances than *Blasted* being the 'true' *Look Back in Anger* for the 1990s. One could even push this conspiracy-theory line of thinking further and suggest that perhaps the indignation of critics like Tinker and Billington over *Blasted* was not entirely heartfelt, more of a case of journalistic sporting, creating an outrage to spice up the otherwise dull January, no critic wanting to be outdone by a colleague in their 'feast of filth' mode of journalism.

This speculation is not to denigrate *Blasted*'s power. It remains a much more rule-breaking piece of writing than Upton's realistic play documenting the violent activity of a group of fourteen-year-old girls. Ultimately, it would be wrong to deny that Kane's premiere played a central role in the theatrical resurgence. Rather, it is interesting to step back, now that we have that luxury, and see how these playwrights were swept up, their differences elided, so that a so-called 'in-yer-face' movement could be born, and furthermore to account for why such an idea remains so powerful, so convincing. With *Blasted*, the theatre of the 1990s was redeemed and the figure of the playwright returned to its former glory. No longer the dud decade, the 1990s were rewritten to be as exciting as '1956 and all that', but as critic and playwright Dan Rebellato skilfully shows in his book of that title, theatre history is never written in an ideological vacuum.[27] Theatrical revolutions that topple the artistic wasteland of 'before' are always involved in a wilful amnesia, repressing, even violently opposing what came before (as in the perceived battle between the 'hard' theatre of John Osborne against the 'soft' plays of Terrence Rattigan and Noël Coward in the 1950s, which Rebellato elucidates).

Borrowing from the past

Blasted can be understood not simply as a revolution but as a continuation of certain strands of dramatic literary tradition. Kane often discussed her influences when working on a play and this invites us to think of her work as borrowing from past writers to create something new. That Kane could speak so clearly about her literary heritage is not surprising; she graduated from Bristol University with a first-class honours degree in drama. *Blasted*, the author stated in interviews, had a number of influences: early Ibsen influenced the first section, Brecht the middle section, and Beckett the final section. She also mentioned Pinter, Bond and Shakespeare as influential in writing the play.[28] Some of these influences might appear surprising at first since the psychological detail of Ibsen or the political epic theatre of Brecht appear far removed from the pared-down intensity of Kane's play. Elaborating on those influences, Kane explained that her goal was 'the detail of Ibsen in terms of situations, combined with Beckett's capacity to go straight to the heart'.[29]

This combination of Ibsen and Beckett can help explain how *Blasted* possesses both specificity and existential abstraction. The early half of *Blasted* is set in an expensive hotel room in Leeds, and Cate and Ian are recognisable characters from this world. Yet the play's second half, following the Soldier's entrance and the bombing of the hotel, transforms that specific world into something more akin to Beckett's desolate landscapes. Beckett, in refusing specificity and cutting off his protagonists from an external world, created characters that can function as representations of our existential plight. We will return to Beckett's influence on Kane's work later in this commentary. Perhaps furthest removed from Kane's play might be Brecht's political theatre, which aimed for dialectical debate and is the touchstone of the critical realist tradition with which Kane's generation was at odds. Yet, as we will see later in this commentary, her play does deal with the political context of war and its relationship to masculinity, even if it refuses to present a clear moral perspective on that subject. Ultimately, Brecht's 'A-effect' or 'making strange' aimed to return the power of interpretation to the audience, to make the theatre audience feel as invested as if they were watching a boxing match, and that 'experiential' quality of Brecht fits nicely with Kane's aesthetic.

Kane's stripped-down dialogue also shows the influence of Edward Bond and Harold Pinter, and recognising those influences helps illuminate Kane's specific use of subtext in this play. She remarked that the first draft of *Blasted* was 'full of huge dense monologues about characters' backgrounds and every feeling was stated, every thought spoken'.[30] Friend Vincent O'Connell gave Kane a copy of Edward Bond's *Saved* (1965) and re-reading Bond's sparse dialogue, in which characters speak only a few words but are able to communicate personal and social worlds, helped Kane develop her own style, which she deemed more 'emotional' than 'intellectual'. Pinter's early plays are a textbook example of the powerful use of subtext, where the meaning of the line comes from that disparity between what is said and what is actually being communicated in the act of saying. Pinter expands upon this idea in his essay 'Writing for the Theatre' (1962):

> So often, below the word spoken, is the thing known and unspoken. My characters tell me so much and no more, with reference to their experience, their aspirations, their motives, their history. Between my lack of a biographical data about them and the ambiguity of what they say lies a territory which is not only worthy of exploration but which it is compulsory to explore. You and I, the characters which grow on a page, most of the time we're inexpressive, giving little away, unreliable, elusive, evasive, obstructive, unwilling.

> But it's out of the attributes that a language arises. A
> language, I repeat, where under what is said, another thing
> is being said.[31]

This 'language' is what we call subtext, and because characters
are always playing a game of subterfuge, of 'giving little
away', the true meaning of what is spoken on stage comes
from 'under what is said' rather than what is directly stated by
the characters. Kane, in stripping down the language of Cate
and Ian, creates a play in which 'the thing known', to use
Pinter's words, is often 'unspoken'. That is why so much of
Kane's dialogue is open to various interpretations.

Her frequent use of a character cutting off a sentence in
mid-thought demonstrates Pinter's and Bond's subtextual
language. Ian, for instance, when asking Cate if she is scared
of dying, says, 'You're young. When I was your age – '. Ian
decides to not finish that recollection. What is more important
than the content of that specific memory is that he will not
reveal it to Cate, perhaps because it reinforces his own age, his
own sense of impending death, something which genuinely
frightens him, or perhaps he does not complete the thought
because he is only willing to let Cate have access to part of his
life, creating a barrier between them by denying her information
about his time as a younger and healthier man. Both readings
are supported by the text. Another example is when the Soldier,
speaking about his dead girlfriend Col, tells Ian, 'Close my
eyes and think about her. She's – '. The Soldier repeats that
interrupted 'she's – ' seven times; each interruption could be a
different thought about Col that the Soldier cannot articulate
aloud, a repeated attempt to describe his dead lover to Ian, or
perhaps he is remembering what happened to her at the hands
of the enemy soldiers. Regardless of what he wants to say
about her, it does not escape his lips because the trauma of
Col's loss is too great. An actor playing that role would have to
finish those sentences in his head, but the audience would only
understand the meaning of those seven interrupted 'she's – '
through what is not said. Kane encouraged actors in rehearsal
to try and find as many interpretations as possible and play
them all, even if such a feat was difficult, if not impossible.

Another influence on *Blasted* was Shakespeare's *King Lear*
(*c.* 1603–1606). The 'thematic similarities' between Kane's
play and Shakespeare's were present from the start of the
writing, but as Kane told Graham Saunders, it was not until
the play's third draft that she became aware of her play's
connections with *King Lear*.[32] Making the connections explicit
allowed Kane to see the importance of Ian's blinding: '[Since]
Ian was a tabloid journalist, it was a kind of castration,
because obviously if you're a reporter your eyes are actually
your main organ.'[33] Thinking about Shakespeare's play also
allowed Kane to solve the problem of writing Scene Four: 'I
struggled with Scene Four for a long time. It was a void in the
play – and I knew something went in there. I just couldn't
think what. And then it dropped into my head. "It's Ian's
Dover scene."'[34] The famous Dover scene invoked by Kane
concerns the meeting of Gloucester and Edgar, father and
son, on the cliffs. Now blind, Gloucester meets the estranged
Edgar, who disguises himself as a beggar called 'Poor Tom'.
Gloucester asks 'Poor Tom' to help him commit suicide by
leading him to the edge of the cliff. Edgar pretends to assist his
father in the act, but leads him to a field instead of the clifftop,
and following Gloucester's brief descent Edgar assures his
father, 'Thy life's a miracle. Speak yet again.'[35] This thwarted
suicide is similar to the interaction in Scene Four between Ian
and Cate, when the blind Ian desires to shoot himself and
Cate gives him the gun, but only after she has removed all the
bullets. Cate claims it was God's will, though the audience
knows the truth.[36] (This is a scene we will return to later in the
commentary.)

Kane's rewriting of moments from *King Lear* demonstrates
her classical aspirations as a writer. Unlike fellow writers such as
Ravenhill or Upton, Kane kept her plays free of contemporary
references that would potentially 'date' them, and confirms her
interest in more universal themes such as love or the possibility
of redemption. This invocation of Shakespeare's play also
connects *Blasted* to the revenge tragedies popular in the late
Elizabethan and Jacobean periods. As many historians have
noted, Queen Elizabeth's final years and James's ascendancy
to the throne in 1603 marked a change in the character of

England; there was a shift from the certainty of religion and custom to a mood of doubt and anxiety. Some literary critics speculate that the literature of the time reflects that cultural shift. Unlike the tragedies of ancient Greece, the revenge tragedies of the early seventeenth century bring violence onstage in all its gory detail, and the revenge plot, in which justice must be meted out for a crime, is governed not by religious belief but by a general attitude of scepticism coupled with an 'eye-for-an-eye' style of retribution. The plays also focus more on the individual consequences of violence and emphasise sexual politics; incest and sexual coupling between royalty and servants, for instance, occur frequently in the plays of John Webster and John Ford.

What disturbed critics of the eighteenth and nineteenth centuries was the refusal to condemn the actions of the characters in these plays, and blame is never cast solely on one character. Given its complicated plot and focus on a royal family, *King Lear* is perhaps not typical of revenge tragedy in the same way as *Hamlet* (*c.* 1599–1601) or Middleton's *The Revenger's Tragedy* (1606); and yet, as critics have pointed out, revenge fuels Lear's wrath, Gloucester's blinding occurs onstage, and the plot revolves around a series of retributions, all leading to the destruction of the majority of the characters.[37] *Blasted*, with its emphasis on bodily defilement, its refusal to moralise and its detailing of the effects of violence on the individual, can be read as 'neo-Jacobean', and the play's emergence at the heart of the 1990s, shortly before the Tory government of John Major was replaced by Tony Blair and a New Labour regime that would eventually disappoint the Left, parallels the uncertain and restless mood of the early seventeenth century. This invocation of the Jacobean theatre is even more evident in Kane's next two plays: *Phaedra's Love*, which uses Seneca's version of the myth as a touchstone for a play about a decadent royal family, and *Cleansed*, which concerns an amoral doctor figure and an incestuous brother and sister.

Yet Kane's reworking of Shakespeare in *Blasted* again connects the play back to Kane's heroes: Beckett, Bond and Barker. Jan Kott's influential essay '*King Lear* or *Endgame*' (collected in his *Shakespeare Our Contemporary* in 1964) argued that the sufferings of Beckett's characters have their origin in Shakespeare's tragedy. 'Edgar leading Gloucester to the precipice at Dover,' Kott argues, '[...] is just the theme of *Endgame*; Beckett was the first to see it in *King Lear*; he eliminated all action, everything external, and repeated it in its skeletal form.'[38] Peter Brook's famous 1962 staging of *King Lear* used Kott's ideas as the bedrock for his interpretation for the Royal Shakespeare Company with Paul Scofield in the title role (it was made into a film in 1971). Brook's staging, which imagined Shakespeare's tragedy on a white, largely empty stage, no doubt influenced the so-called 'New Jacobeans' Bond and Barker, and their retellings of the Shakespeare tragedy, in Bond's *Lear* (1971) and Barker's *Seven Lears* (1989). Barker notably describes his 'theatre of catastrophe' as 'a modern form of tragedy', and his desire to create 'theatre without a conscience' that abolishes the 'routine distinctions between good and bad actions' manifests itself in Kane's plays.[39]

Having placed Kane's play in a theatrical context, both in terms of her contemporaries and her antecedents, the commentary will now focus more specifically on the content of the play. Arguably, *Blasted* grapples with key issues that were at the forefront in the 1990s, and in many ways remain in our global consciousness in this new century – issues such as war, masculinity and the possibility of ethics in the face of devastating violence. This discussion of the play's content will give the reader one road map for navigating the play, and provide some potential answers to the questions listed at the start of this commentary, though again it bears repeating that these answers are partial rather than definitive. Interspersed with these more philosophical ideas will be discussions of the play in performance, specifically three major productions of *Blasted* in the first decade of the twenty-first century: James Macdonald's 2001 revival at the Royal Court Downstairs, the New York premiere at Soho Rep in 2008, and Sean Holmes's 2010 revival at the Lyric, Hammersmith. Any reader of Kane's work must make the hard leap of imagining the plays on stage and these thoughts might prove useful to directors, actors and designers hoping to tackle a production of *Blasted*.

The logic of war

Kane was especially reticent to interpret her work, writing no Prefaces or Author's Notes, except for a brief afterword to the first publication of *Blasted* in the *Frontline Intelligence 2* anthology. But as we have seen, Kane often spoke at length about her work in interviews and in conversation with critics and fellow writers, and these documents give us an insight into the genesis of *Blasted*.

Kane began writing the play on 30 March 1993. At first, it was solely about the troubled relationship between Ian and Cate, and the rape that Cate suffers at Ian's hands in the hotel room in Leeds during the blackout between the two scenes. During work on that first draft, however, global events intervened and this had a profound impact on the writing of *Blasted*. Kane told Aleks Sierz:

> At some point during the first couple of weeks writing,
> I switched on the television. Srebrenica was under siege.
> I was suddenly disinterested in the play I was writing. What
> I wanted to write about was what I'd just seen on TV.[40]

Kane elaborated on this incident in an interview with Graham Saunders. She describes specifically seeing a seventy-year-old Muslim woman begging for help during the evening news and that 'extreme pain' was something that made Kane eventually include the Soldier in her 'domestic' play about Ian and Cate. Kane would eventually remove all specific references to Serbia from the play, and yet it is worth considering the conflict that inspired Kane to transform her initial story, even if ultimately the play should not be understood as a play *about* that conflict.

The attack on Srebrenica was the beginning of what would become the largest mass murder in Europe since the systematic killings perpetuated by the Nazis during the Second World War. Starting in 1992, the Bosnian Serbs sought to achieve racial 'integrity' in the region following the republic's declaration of independence from Yugoslavia. The Serbs began a campaign of 'ethnic cleansing' against the Bosniaks, better known in the West as the Bosnian Muslims or simply Bosnians. During this time, Srebrenica and the surrounding villages came under constant attack from the Serbian military; and in July 1995 Srebrenica became the site of genocide when the Serbs massacred at least 8,000 Muslim boys and men. Another part of the Serbian campaign was the use of rape as a weapon of war, and in the figures tallying the number of deaths, the number of Bosnian woman raped during the conflict remains largely unaccounted.

In the second draft of the play, started in June 1993, Ian encounters Vladek, a soldier who enters the hotel room and takes Ian at gunpoint.[41] In this draft, the Soldier is specifically identified as Serbian. He speaks his 'own language' outside the door, thus prompting Ian to mutter, 'Speak the Queen's fucking English, you fucking nigger shit.' Vladek tells Ian, 'This is a Serbian town now. Where's your passport?' Thus, the hotel room in Leeds is transported to a specifically Serbian war zone.

One of the allures of the modern-day hotel room is its anonymity; its appearance is nearly indistinguishable between one western country and the next. Regardless of where the hotel is located, the standardisation of the hotel room cuts it off from what is occurring outside. As Kane's opening stage direction indicates, the room 'is so expensive it could be anywhere in the world'. But while it could be 'anywhere in the world', the speech of Ian and Cate locates it firmly in 1990s England (Cate's South London accent and love of football, Ian's continual use of racist British slang terms for immigrants). But with the entrance of Vladek, the unity of space is disrupted. The hotel room is transported; the outside is no longer the banal city of Leeds, but the horror show of Srebrenica.

When *Blasted* opened at the Royal Court Theatre Upstairs in January 1995, however, the play had undergone a crucial change.[42] Kane stripped all identifiable ethnic designations from the play. The soldier is no longer called Vladek; in fact, he is never given a proper name. When he breaks into the hotel, instead of designating the nationality of the invading troops, he simply tells Ian, 'Our town now,' and that 'our' is never defined except that it is definitively not 'English.' Descriptions of the violent conflict conjure images of the Bosnian genocide, and yet they can also be seen to describe other atrocities of the times – the Rwandan genocide of 1994, for instance – and for a present-day audience the eruption of violence in an expensive hotel room might be uncannily reminiscent of the November 2008 al-Qaida attacks on the hotels in Mumbai. In removing those specific details, Kane unmoored her play from the 1990s and made it resonate beyond its specific origins in the Serbian campaign of 'ethnic cleansing'.

In performance, the ambiguity of the Soldier's identity can lead to a particular challenge for the actor playing that role. In the London productions, the Soldier has tended to have an Irish accent. Sean Holmes, director of the 2010 revival at the Lyric, Hammersmith, explains this choice for the Soldier:

> What is interesting is that the Soldier in each of the previous two main British productions has been Irish [Dermot Kerrigan in 1995, Tom Jordan Murphy in 2001]. I was determined [the Soldier] wouldn't be [Irish] in mine. And then Aiden [Kelly] – who is from Dublin – was the best person we saw, so [the Soldier] ended up being Irish again. Maybe that slight sense of difference releases something in the part. Any accent too 'other' would diminish the threat of the Soldier. He could be any one of us.[43]

Having the Soldier sound not completely 'other' emphasises how these productions sought to make the Soldier not an agent of 'foreign' violence, but something closer to home. In Holmes's opinion, that choice prevents the London audience from 'locating' and 'distancing the events' that the Soldier describes.

The 2008 New York premiere took a different approach. Louis Cancelmi, who is 'part Lebanese, part Czech and part Italian', played the Soldier. During the first read-through, he tried the Soldier's lines 'in his own [American] accent', but both he and director Sarah Benson found that choice to be loaded and not 'faithful' to the text. This feeling was due in large part to the fact that the actors playing Ian and Cate would speak with the original English accents as designated in the play. Through the rehearsal process Cancelmi 'grounded the character vocally in the Balkans and former Eastern bloc nations':

I listened to a wide range of people from that part of the world to create a distinctly foreign but not readily *placeable* voice. The main sounds were all Slavic: Georgian, Chechnyan, Estonian, Macedonian, Serbo-Croatian. I don't think any group of people actually speaks with the accent I ended up creating for the play, but the idea was that some individual somewhere might.[44]

In some ways, this choice harkens back to Kane's early drafts, where the Soldier was specifically Serbian. The choice also reflects that, to many American ears, a British and Irish accent are not easily distinguishable, so Holmes's rationale would not make sense to an audience in New York. Yet Cancelmi's accent was less specifically tied to a place than to a region. What was specific about this production's Soldier was he was clearly part of a civil conflict. Teresa Squire's costume for the Soldier featured track pants and a soccer T-shirt to which a piece of camouflage was added. This soldier was not a professional, not the product of basic training; in Cancelmi's words, 'The war came to him.'

In the same way, the war comes to Ian. A 'huge explosion' rocks the hotel room shortly after the Soldier's introduction. It is a stage moment that announces to the audience that the presumed sense of protection provided by the 'anonymous' hotel room has been destroyed. Has the unthinkable happened and a 'foreign' force invaded Leeds? Imagine the headline, written by one of Ian's colleagues: 'Neighbouring Soldiers Attack Leeds!' Recall that before the Soldier's appearance, Cate remarks to Ian, upon glancing out of the hotel window, 'Looks like there's a war on.' At that moment in the play, Cate appears to be speaking metaphorically – urban blight seen as a violent conflict akin to war. But has simile become reality? And if so, is the hotel room no longer in Leeds, but transported to an actual war zone, uprooted to a place like Srebrenica in 1995 or Baghdad in 2003? *Blasted* makes the answer to this question purposefully unclear because, perhaps, ultimately it doesn't matter, since the effect is the same. What we hope is impossible – a civil conflict in a 'first-world' country – has become a reality for Ian and Cate. For many directors, this is why the 'huge explosion' is such a major event in the play: it marks the transition from the real into a nightmare or new reality. But the play's ambiguity renders even that simple opposition fuzzy: could it all be a nightmare or, more challenging yet, could the play's second half be the real and the first half the dream?

Two possible approaches to staging the blast are exemplified by the 2001 revival and the 2008 New York production: the first could be classified as 'realistic', while the second could be described as more 'expressionistic' or 'abstract'.

James Macdonald told his assistant director on the 2001 revival at the Royal Court, Joseph Hill-Gibbins, that the explosion was pivotal and that staging the play in the larger downstairs space meant that more could be made of the moment than when the play was done on a smaller budget in the Upstairs space in 1995. But the difference between the two productions was more a question of scale. What Macdonald's 1995 and 2001 productions emphasised was the arrival of war in the mundane city of Leeds. We witnessed the effects of an actual mortar explosion 'blasting' the hotel room. The realistic components of the room remained but the stage picture now looked like a photograph that might accompany a *New York Times* or *Guardian* article on the ravages of war. The Royal Court's promotional and educational materials also framed the play as a response to the Serbian conflict, and that affected my own watching of the play.

The New York production, on the other hand, made the explosion a crucial event by having it redefine the space in a highly inventive way. It was a more 'abstracted' blast than in the Macdonald production. The hotel room, though created with a careful degree of verisimilitude by set designer Louisa Thompson, became a space that, following the loud explosion and blackout, defied logic. In the darkness, the hotel floor moved back, taking with it what it would, while all the appliances remained hanging there, stripped of their original context. When the lights came up for Scene Three, the actual theatre floor as well as the theatre walls, backstage and the truss and pulley system were all revealed, and the only anchor was the back wall of the hotel room. It was, in the words of director

Sarah Benson, 'a real mess every night' rather than a 'clever' set built to look like an exploded hotel room. Benson explains:

> [The blast] is the point where the play itself breaks apart formally to accommodate the massiveness of the events Sarah is writing about. So we wanted it to start out feeling very much like a presentational theatre set which then transformed during the blast into a much more open space that was shared by the play and the audience, so that it became civic. Another thing we learned during tech was how important it was that the explosion happens in a blackout. The play is called *Blasted* not *Blasting* and it's classical in that sense. The change is unseen. You experience the result.[45]

The result of this design was that the audience's sense of space was radically dislocated when the lights returned. It wasn't just that the hotel room was 'blasted' but that the entire theatre had come undone, and we were situated inside the destruction. One audience member commented that they spent the first few moments of Scene Three trying to work out what had happened to the space because their eyes couldn't 'read' it. We were clearly no longer in a hotel room in Leeds, or even, perhaps, in a 'real' physical location, but instead had been transported to some place that was completely unfamiliar; and, crucially, we were there with the play's three characters.

Director Sean Holmes's 2010 production took a similar approach. Inspired by a German production, Holmes describes the hotel room after the blast in his production like this: 'We removed all the walls after the blast, leaving only the floor and the bed and some detritus. Around it was the exposed superstructure of the hotel.'[46] While not as metatheatrical as the New York production, the effect of removing the walls entirely and exposing the hotel's frame hollowed out the room; the traces of the hotel remain, but it has been transformed into a metaphorical space. Holmes feels that the play's second half 'has the logic of nightmare and that it is almost as if the nightmares of the three characters intersect'.[47] The skeletal outline of the hotel reminds the audience of what occurred in that hotel room in the play's first half (Cate's rape, for instance) and yet now the space is the site of a nightmarish civil war, that may or may not exist in the minds of the characters.

You could argue that Benson's and Holmes's productions are more truthful to the final version of the play, emphasising the confusion of worlds. But could the opposite also be true? Macdonald's staging realistically blasted the hotel room in Leeds with a mortar bomb, reinforcing that it is the *same* hotel room in Leeds that has become the site of a war. Might not that directorial approach more accurately capture Kane's intent? Yet, given the purposeful ambiguity of the text, both approaches are valid, and no doubt future directors and designers will find new 'solutions' to the challenges raised by Kane's stage directions. But what all three productions highlight is the radical shift that takes place in the play following the blast, and this is worth considering in more detail.

The universal: Kane, Pinter and Beckett

Regardless of the directorial interpretation, the play's setting, following the blast, functions as a metaphorical third space, both Leeds and a war zone, while crucially neither. The choice of stripping away the specific ethnic designations for the Soldier and the destruction of the hotel room by a mortar bomb means that the play's second half takes place in a context that is neither domestic or international, but somehow both at the same time. As a result, *Blasted* becomes an allegory about violence more than a play about a specific act of violence.

As discussed earlier, the work of Beckett and Pinter influenced *Blasted*, and a move to a more universal dimension can be found in Pinter's *One for the Road* and Beckett's *Catastrophe*. It can be helpful to look at these two plays alongside Kane's.

A statement of seduction and torture occurring in an unnamed country in four brief scenes, Pinter's *One for the Road* (1984) shows Nicolas, a loquacious sadist, interrogating a family while his unseen men commit vicious acts on them. Except for the suggestion that Victor may be an intellectual and that his wife Gila's father was a government official, nothing else is known about the family or its 'crimes' against the state. Nicolas is deeply uninterested in determining motive or allowing them to reveal information about their beliefs. Each scene of the play is a virtual monologue delivered by Nicolas to a largely silent member of the family, while the others are confined in 'another room', where they are purportedly violated. The enclosed space of Nicolas's office becomes an everywhere – not a far-removed geographical location but a metaphor. Violence begets violence *in toto* and the implication of *One for the Road* is that Nicolas represents not a specific figure, not a stand-in for Pinochet or Milosevic, but one of the Nicolases who are to be found everywhere. His actions represent the workings of repressive power found not just abroad, but in our homelands as well.

In a similar fashion, Beckett's short play *Catastrophe* (1982) recounts a director's rehearsal in which his assistant manipulates a protagonist, mute and motionless, into an image, a 'castastrophe', that will have the audience 'on their feet'.[48] The shivering body of the protagonist, his flesh 'whitened', is first lit, and then on cue all lights go to black, with only one source remaining to illuminate the scalp of the figure, transforming his face into a void. The play was dedicated to the Czech playwright, reformer and future-president Václav Havel, who was imprisoned for four and a half years for 'subversion'. As part of his sentence, Havel was forbidden to write. Though dedicated to Havel and first performed at the 1982 Avignon Festival as part of 'A Night for Václav Havel', *Catastrophe* never mentions any specific events relating to Havel's treatment in communist Czechoslovakia.

On one level, the play can be read as Beckett's metatheatrical comment on the power dynamics of his own stage images, which rendered actors' bodies immobile (*Happy Days*, *Play*), largely mute (*Rockabye*) or reduced to a speaking mouth (*Not I*). But it can also be read as a political allegory. The spectacles of power in totalitarian states render its prisoners not merely speechless, but also invisible, for Beckett equates the face, specifically the eyes, with one's individuality, and the erasure of the Protagonist's face in *Catastrophe* is the director's goal in manipulating the Protagonist's body in order to give the audience a spectacle that they will applaud: 'Let 'em have it,' the Director exclaims as Luke the lighting technician prepares to darken the Protagonist's features. Yet the Protagonist, in a gesture of resistance, raises his head in the final instant against the wishes of the Director, who mocked his assistant at the suggestion of such an act, and that revelation of the Protagonist's gaze, a reminder of his humanity, silences the applauding crowd, because instead of a faceless void they see a person. Beckett, never prone to explaining his work, had this to say about the play's final image: '[The Protagonist's] saying: You bastards, you haven't finished me yet!'[49]

Pinter's and Beckett's plays both index the specific historical situations that inspired them. For Beckett, it is Havel's imprisonment; for Pinter, it is his involvement in uncovering human rights abuses through his work with organisations such as International PEN and Amnesty International. Yet the plays are not reducible to a dramatisation of those specific issues, and by rendering the subject matter allegorical rather than descriptive, and seeing the plays performed in different contexts, at different historical moments, the viewer is able to personalise the material. To an American audience in 2010, for instance, Pinter's *One for the Road* could be read as a comment on the US military's interrogation techniques in Iraq and Afghanistan. That is to say, the play takes on new resonances by not being reducible to a specific historical incident, but those resonances are also changeable.

It is the same with Kane's play. But how can we potentially read the violence of *Blasted* as an allegory, as a symbol for something else? What politically is Kane's play 'saying' in representing such extreme violence which neither Pinter's nor Beckett's plays dare to show?

The logic of rape

The structure of *Blasted* carefully creates parallel incidents between the play's first and second halves:

Scene Two: Ian and Cate

[**Cate**] *takes the gun from* [**Ian**'s] *holster and points it at his groin. He backs off rapidly.*

Ian   Easy, easy, that's a loaded gun.

Cate   I d- d- d- d- d- d- d- d- d-

Ian   Catie, come on.

Cate   d- d- d- d- d- d- d- d- d- d-

Ian   You don't want an accident. Think about your mum. And your brother. What would they think?

Cate   I d- d- d- d- d- d- d- d- d- d- d- d- d-

Cate *trembles and starts gasping for air.*

She faints.

Ian *goes to her, takes the gun and* [. . .] *lies her on the bed on her back.*

He puts the gun to her head, lies between her legs, and simulates sex.

As he comes, **Cate** *sits bolt upright with a shout.*

Scene Three: Ian and the Soldier

Soldier   Turn over, Ian.

Ian   Why?

Soldier   Going to fuck you.

Ian   No.

Soldier   Kill you then.

Ian   Fine.

Soldier   See. Rather be shot than fucked and shot.

Ian   Yes.

[. . .]

[**The Soldier**] *pulls down* **Ian**'s *trousers, undoes his own and rapes him – eyes closed and smelling* **Ian**'s *hair.*

The **Soldier** *is crying his heart out.*

Ian's *face registers pain, but he is silent.*

When the **Soldier** *has finished he pulls up his trousers and pushes the revolver up* **Ian***'s anus.*

Soldier   Bastard pulled the trigger on [my girlfriend] Col. What's it like?

Ian   (*Tries to answer. He can't.*)

Soldier   (*Withdraws the gun and sits next to* **Ian**.)

You never fucked by a man before?

Ian   (*Doesn't answer.*)

Soldier   Didn't think so. It's nothing. Saw thousands of people packing into trucks like pigs trying to leave town. Women threw their babies on board hoping someone would look after them. Crushing each other to death. Insides of people's heads came out of their eyes. Saw a child most of his face blown off, [. . .] starving man eating his dead wife's leg. Gun was born here and won't die. Can't get tragic about your arse.

In the first quote, the audience witnesses the first rape to be seen on stage. Here, Ian imposes himself on Cate while she is unconscious during a fit, using her docile body in a masturbatory way. This moment is a stand-in for Cate's far more violent rape that occurs during the blackout between Scenes One and Two, one of the few moments of violence in the play not to be seen on stage. Of that rape, we only see the consequences: the scattered remains of the flowers, talk of Cate's bleeding orifices. The first moment quoted above functions metonymically for the unseen rape. But even taken in tandem, those events at first appear individuated: one man's cruel act against a woman who looks up to him almost as if he were her father. But that changes when it is juxtaposed with the next extract quoted above. The Soldier's rape of Ian – during which he sodomises Ian with his penis and then repeats the act using Ian's own revolver – is rendered symbolic, a representation of the violence occurring outside the hotel room. The Soldier tells Ian what soldiers did to his girlfriend Col. Again, crucially, we do not 'see' what happens to Col on stage. But then the Soldier re-enacts that violation on Ian's body. The repetition of rape – the description of Col's rape by soldiers, the staging of Ian's rape by the Soldier, which is then repeated using the gun – transforms individual acts into allegorical symbols, Ian's rape standing in for all the genocidal events described by the soldier. Ian's violated body becomes the means by which the atrocities occurring outside become visible.

We can't 'see' what the Soldier sees because the stage cannot represent the horrors of 'ethnic cleansing' on its actual scale. Yet we come to understand that violence when we witness the rape of Ian. The Soldier tells Ian after his violation: 'Can't get tragic about your arse.' What is tragic, however, is how the play's structure – the mirroring of the two rapes – renders any single act of violence into a pattern. That is to say, in *Blasted*, no rape occurs in isolation; there is a logic that connects them. The consequence of the metaphorisation of Ian's rape is that Cate's rape earlier in the play retrospectively becomes symbolic: part and parcel of the same violent causal chain.

What *Blasted* does is articulate the coherence between individual acts of rape and the use of rape in the strategic planning of war. Kane stated in an interview: '"What does a common rape in Leeds have to do with mass rape in Bosnia?" And the answer appears to be "Quite a lot." '[50] This is a statement that she extended elsewhere: 'The logical conclusion of the attitude that produces an isolated rape in England is the rape camps in Bosnia, and the logical conclusion to the way society expects men to behave is war.'[51] In Kane's view, violence is omnipresent, and *Blasted* suggests that a culture that sanctions mass murder abroad inevitably allows crimes of rape to occur at home. Ian is no different from a soldier, Serbian or otherwise; for what they share is the universal logic of violence, and that logic exists during moments of 'peace' just as it does in war; at the very least, the rationale of war and 'ethnic cleansing' are reflected in 'mundane' occurrences like a 'common' rape.

While this move towards universalising her analysis of violence connects Kane to Pinter and Beckett, the radical difference lies in the scenes of physical violence. Like Pinter's *One for the Road*, *Blasted* sets out not to stage a specific historical incident by narrating barbarity in a specific geographical locale, but rather affirms the presence of violence everywhere. Globalisation has greatly intensified the interdependent relationship between the local and the faraway. Kane's play links the logic of 'common' rape to the atrocities occurring abroad or in the so-called 'developing world'. In Pinter's play, however, violence is always figured linguistically. Gila is raped by Nicolas's men, but we know this only because Nicolas asks her; Victor's tongue is cut out, but we only see the effects: Victor's inability to respond to Nicolas's questions in the final scene. But in *Blasted* violence is not represented through language; it occurs on stage in front of the audience's eyes. Pinter once confessed to Kane that the violence of her plays 'frightened the shit' out of him, to which Kane playfully responded, 'There's some things you just can't take, Harold.' [52] The violence that Pinter will not show, those 'things' that Kane teased him he 'couldn't take', Kane forces us to see: the damaged body is centre stage in *Blasted*.

The violence of men

Bound up with the play's illumination of the logic of war is its examination of masculinity. In the previous section, we touched on how the play draws parallels between sexual violence in a domestic context and its use as a weapon during wartime. In *Blasted*, it is crucial to note that it is men who carry out those crimes. Ian is the character through whom the play most clearly dramatises the contradictions of a dominant strand of late-twentieth-century 'straight' masculinity. The playwright David Edgar concludes that 'the decline of the dominant role of men – in the workplace and in the family – is probably the biggest single story of the last thirty years in the western countries'.[53] In response to the perceived reduction of power, masculinity policed its boundaries with a renewed vigour in the 1990s.

The beginning of the twenty-first century in the industrialised world has seen the popular phenomenon of the 'metrosexual' – the urbane heterosexual guy who isn't afraid to pluck his eyebrows and get facials – coupled with the general decline of homophobia, especially among young men. The 1990s, however, were more ambivalent about a male identity that was no longer dominant, lacked father figures, and needed to appropriate the fetishised masculinity of affluent gay culture (the rituals of bodybuilding and the gym, the importance of appearance) in order to validate their perceived waning power. The rise of 'lad culture' in the 1990s did not merely reflect the decline of male economic power (though that is not a trivial issue by any means), but also the perceived weakening of masculinity because of its 'femininisation.' Or to put it another way, there was a fear that men were no longer 'men'. A world where men look up to other men's bodies creates pleasures coupled with fear, for that idolatry can easily slip into homosexuality. It is, therefore, unsurprising that the playwrights of the late 1990s wanted to tell and retell stories about the relationships between men. *Blasted* is a great example of this fascination with masculinity.

Ian is a journalist who does not cover 'foreign affairs' and is uninterested in writing about the violence that the Soldier describes. What Ian does is write 'stories' that have to be 'personal': 'Shootings and rapes and kids getting fiddled by queer priests and schoolteachers.' The story that Ian relays to his colleague over the phone concerns a female British tourist who is murdered by a serial killer in an isolated New Zealand forest. Though Ian describes his work as 'personal', the truth is that his reporting is obsessed with male violence. He takes delight in narrating the details of tourist Samantha Scrace's violent end to his fellow male reporter, concluding his dictation with a personal anecdote about a 'Scouse tart' who spreads 'her legs' but is ultimately 'not worth the space'. If Ian's subject is 'personal' tales of male violence, Ian could himself be his own subject: his rape of Cate in the hotel room and his violent dismissal of women as not 'worth' much make him little better than the criminals featured in his tabloid reporting.

Ian is also more than simply a passive reporter of homeland violence. There are intimations that he has worked for the British Security Service (MI5) and has spied on, even murdered those perceived to be disloyal to Britain: 'Done the jobs they asked. Because I love this land,' and going so far as to declare

himself a 'Killer' at the climax of oral sex. His supposed 'love
of country' is made manifest by his frequent use of racist
invective. He fears that Leeds is 'turning into Wogland', and
when Cate reprimands him for his casual racism, he asks if she
is a 'nigger-lover'. In Kane's play, Ian's racism and the violence
that accompanies it emerge from the same source: a fear that
England is no longer the England of fantastical memory, a
pure England that is racially and ethnically homogenous –
which of course it never was. The irony is that Ian is not
English but Welsh, and the English occupied Wales for centuries
following a thirteenth-century invasion, an early experiment in
imperialism. To contemporary ears, it sounds ludicrous when
the Soldier asks Ian if he would die for his country, Wales,
since Wales has long been part of the United Kingdom: it is
one of the play's many moments of humour. In Ian's mind,
'English and Welsh are the same.' Yet the Soldier's questions
about Ian's nationality remind the audience that Ian's
Englishness is far from pure and in the eyes of some, Ian is one
of the 'foreigners' that he is so fond of attacking, one of those
'imported' to England but who will never truly be English.

Ian does not attempt to police racial boundaries alone, but
sexual ones as well. He calls his ex-wife Stella a 'lesbos' and
cannot believe that she could have preferred another woman.
Observing Cate's clothes, he demeans Cate, saying she has the
'potential' for 'sucking gash', a violent image that renders the
female genitalia into a wound. When Cate inquires if Ian has
ever been with a man in a sexual way, he gestures to his penis
and asks, 'How can you think that?', suggesting, perhaps, that
gay men are born without penises, or at least, not very 'manly'
ones; or perhaps he is indicating that Cate caused his member
to achieve an erection, so how could she even suspect he is not
fully heterosexual? Once he hangs up the phone, Ian also
dismisses his male colleague as a 'tosser', a term that equates a
man who takes pleasure in his own body as somehow less of a
'real man' because his self-love makes him 'feminine'. Ian's
comments about sexuality demonstrate the contradiction at the
heart of male heterosexuality: the very thing that men are
supposed to desire is the very thing that many are repelled by.
The solution to this contradictory logic is to conquer the

feminine – to imagine the female body as a battlefield whose conquest separates the male body from any taint of femininity. When Ian assures the Soldier that he has not killed Cate, the Soldier asks, 'Why not, don't seem to like her very much,' to which Ian can only answer, 'I do. She's . . . a woman.' In Ian's logic, women are to be wanted and hated, desired then 'fucked over'.

Kane's play reveals Ian to be not all-powerful – quite the opposite, in fact. His body is failing him; one of his lungs has already been removed and the other one is soon to go; and if the cancer doesn't kill him first, cirrhosis of the liver will. For all of his talk of hatred of women and 'minorities', Ian is a broken man, often reduced to a child. He is embarrassed when Cate talks about the pleasure that she takes in her own sexual desires, and he is humiliated when Cate laughs at his request to 'put [her] mouth on [him]'. Kane's play intimates what sociologist Michael Kimmel describes in his influential 1994 essay 'Masculinity as Homophobia' as the true cause of hatred such as Ian's:

> Homophobia [and by extension, racism as well] is the fear that other men will unmask us, emasculate us, reveal to us and the world that we do not measure up, that we are not real men. We are afraid to let other men see that fear. Fear makes us ashamed, because the recognition of fear in ourselves is proof to ourselves that we are not as manly as we pretend.[54]

Whether alone in the hotel room with Cate or with the Soldier, Ian must constantly convince himself and others of his power: by denigrating people of colour, gays and lesbians. But that power is revealed to be an act. The Soldier brutalises Ian in a way that Ian could not even fathom, while Cate outsmarts him, biting his beloved penis and escaping, only to return at the play's end to take care of him.

Men cannot be nurturers in *Blasted*. Ian is a father, but his own son Matthew will not speak to him, and his divorce from his wife Stella was clearly not amicable. Cate's 'fits', when she faints and speaks things that she cannot remember, begin after her father returns, as if his reappearance in her life triggers psychic turmoil. The mention of her father suggests that Cate's continued relationship with Ian potentially stems from a desire for an older, male caregiver. Yet Ian cannot truly care for her. Instead, he manipulates Cate's need for affirmation to his own advantage so that he can achieve sexual gratification. But Ian needs Cate to be his caregiver, at least when this does not deflate his 'masculinity'. Ian enjoys Cate's being 'soft' with him alone in the hotel, but he is embarrassed when his phone calls with her are being monitored and he knows that men could be listening to Cate saying that she loves him.

The Soldier acts similarly. He grieves for the death of his beloved 'Col', but the means by which he marks that loss is to rape Ian and eat his eyes. The man who at the start of the play announces that he has 'shat in better places' than this hotel is no more than a blind head protruding from that same hotel's floorboards by the play's end. We witness the price of a view of masculinity that is bereft of nurturing and conflicted by its need and repulsion for the feminine: the image of the Soldier's corpse left to rot in the hotel room and, most important, of Ian's wounded face, one of the play's most iconic images.

The possibility of ethics

The conclusion of Kane's *Blasted* reminds us how radical Kane's work is. It can also give those of us making theatre some ideas about how the art form can continue to develop in the coming decades. That may appear a strange claim. When the subject of the 'future of theatre' is raised, the conversation usually revolves around how the old-fashioned medium of the stage must integrate new technologies such as video and the web in order to get the 'kids' into the seats. But I want to take a different tack, and show how *Blasted* is the kind of theatre that is experiential while also refusing to give up engagement with the larger social world. To put it another way, *Blasted* is an experientially political play, a kind of political theatre that functions not pedagogically but affectively. And this facet of Kane's work might be part of the reason why her plays continue to resonate so much with younger theatregoers, who 'got' Kane's work before many critics did. To unpack this idea, we have to return to the subject that we began with: the controversy surrounding the first production of *Blasted*.

Critics who attacked *Blasted* were not merely angry at the play's violence. Looking back, it is worthwhile noting that though the Left-leaning *Guardian* and tabloid *Daily Mail* were on the same page about Kane's play, they had different motivations for disliking it. The *Guardian*'s Michael Billington called the play 'naive tosh' not because he thought that made good copy, but because he believed that the play 'failed' to engage with the social world, or in his words, it was not 'based on exact social observation'. And although he revised his opinion of the play by the time of its 2001 revival, he still felt that its lack of a specific social world rendered it 'flawed'. Supporters of Kane's play, eager to challenge Billington and others, couched their ripostes in clear moral terms of right and wrong, their line of argument being that, far from being amoral, *Blasted* carried quite a moral message, despite the violence. Such a response relies often on a wilful re-reading. It sees this play through the lens of the critical realist tradition of earlier British theatre that transforms ambiguity into certainty. Such a misreading reduces the profound differences between the world view of 1990s theatre and the work of previous generations.

Kane herself said, contrary to the 'party line' that the then-Artistic Director Stephen Daldry and the Royal Court Theatre were selling: 'I don't think *Blasted* is a moral play – I think it is amoral, and that is one of the reasons people got terribly upset.'[55] This is a position to which Kane returned, telling Aleks Sierz in January 1999:

> There has been a lot of discussion about the morality of
> the play [*Blasted*], which I find just as inappropriate as the
> accusations of immorality. Morality doesn't come into it.
> I thought it was amoral. It doesn't sloganise, it doesn't have
> a moral or political programme.[56]

Ultimately, Kane's critics are correct: *Blasted* is not political (and by extension, not feminist) in any *traditional* sense. No programme is espoused; no solutions are proposed; characters do not represent any clear divide between good and evil, victim and victimiser; there is no clear message, no commitment to a specific goal. But that kind of 'amorality' does not preclude engagement.

A 'pure' political theatre – assuming there is such a thing – would be aligned with morality, while Kane's plays instead represent an ethical theatre. An ethical engagement with the world should be distinguished from a moral interpretation. Philosopher Gilles Deleuze makes the distinction between the two concepts this way:

> The difference is that morality presents us with a series of constraining rules of a special sort, ones that judge actions and intentions by considering them in relation to transcendent values (this is good, that's bad . . .); ethics is a set of optional rules that assess what we do, what we say, in relation to the ways of existing involved.[57]

While morality is aligned with law, and actions are evaluated by a set of metaphysical ideals, ethics is contextual; its 'optional rules' assess actions in relation to the here and now, to the material set of circumstances in which we find ourselves. The political activist and philosopher Alain Badiou refines Deleuze's distinction by arguing forcefully that ethics can never be understood in a universal sense. Instead, 'there is', he writes, 'only the ethic-of (of politics, of love, of science, of art)'.[58] For Badiou, the maxim that best encapsulates ethics is, 'Do all that you can to persevere in that which exceeds your perseverance,' which he shortens to, 'Keep going!'[59] This call-to-endurance echoes Beckett's famous dictum that closes his novel *The Unnamable*, 'You must go on, I can't go on, I'll go on.'[60]

For me, Kane's play is, in fact, amoral, but deeply ethical. It teaches us about endurance and shows her characters learning new relationships for existing in a new and horrifying world. This kind of ethics is felt most strongly in the play's moments of humour as well as its hauntingly simple conclusion. I know comedy and Sarah Kane might seem strange bedfellows to some, but Kane loved a good joke. Her friend Elana Greenfield wrote about how Kane spent some of her time in New York

learning how to master the Jewish style of joke-telling
(complete with the necessary 'Jewish shrug' for punctuation),
all of which must have been highly amusing coming from a
girl from Essex.[61] What jokes do best is puncture the balloon of
high-minded ideals with a reminder of the body, of materiality,
of truth. Humour's incongruity does not give us what is
expected, and in subverting expectations jokes make us laugh.
When we expect an air of solemnity, and instead get the stink
of the fart; when we expect a light-hearted chat, and instead
get a vivid description of a mass murder; when we expect
serious investigative reporting, and instead hear a discussion of
hairstyles: frustrated expectations breed comedy. The Jewish
tradition of comedy is all about using laughter in the face of
adversity, and perhaps that is what drew Kane to it. Its
incongruity is to persist, despite everything, with laughter.

Humour punctuates the wounding of bodies in *Blasted*, for
even in this nightmare, Cate and Ian still tell jokes. When Cate
returns to the remnants of the hotel room following the
Soldier's death, she carries a crying baby that a woman gave her.
In 'Ian's Dover scene' (see above), the blind Ian begs Cate to give
him the Soldier's gun so he can finish the job that the Soldier
began. Cate, however, tells him, 'It's wrong to kill yourself'
because 'God wouldn't like it.' Ian's reply: 'No God. No Father
Christmas. No fairies. No Narnia. No fucking nothing.' To
Ian, God is no more real than the fundamentalist fantasies of
a C.S. Lewis novel. Cate and Ian's theological back-and-forth
continues with Cate claiming that God is necessary for life to
have meaning, while Ian takes the Enlightenment high road,
arguing that 'everything's got a scientific explanation.' It is
the classic dispute between religion and science, but the body
undercuts the solemnity of this 'Is There A God' debate.

In the 2001 revival of the play at the Royal Court, actor
Neil Dudgeon's Ian makes his case for science as his eye sockets
bleed, while Cate's plea for metaphysics is undercut by a hungry
baby's cries, with Kelly Reilly delivering her lines as she paces
around the damaged hotel room, desperately looking for
sustenance for the infant. Given the dire circumstances, how
could God's existence even matter? The audience's laughter
came at the debate's conclusion. Cate gives in to Ian's request.

Ian puts the gun in his mouth, but in a rare instance of good manners, he removes the gun and tells Cate, 'Don't stand behind me.' A beat. Then laughter. The tragedy of a man commiting suicide is underscored by the bloody realities of blowing your head off: if Cate stood behind Ian, she would find herself getting very messy. The physical undermines the metaphysical. But there will be no blood, no gore. Ian pulls the trigger and the gun only clicks, empty of bullets. A satisfied Cate tells Ian, 'Fate, see. You're not meant to do it. God – '. But if metaphysics appears to have scored a victory, the audience is in on a joke that Ian literally can't see. Cate herself took the bullets out of the gun, her faith in God's plan not so steadfast. Upon hearing Cate invoke God, Ian hurls the gun and yells, 'The cunt.' Again, laughter. But just as the empty gun hits the floor, Cate realises the baby has died in her arms. And in that moment, laughter ceases, giving way to tragedy. If the truth of the body reasserts itself first to produce humour, it then serves as a reminder of the body's ultimate truth: its eventual demise.

Blasted does not end with the baby's death. There is still one final joke to tell. Cate buries the baby and leaves Ian in a quest for food. Now alone, Ian pursues a final solution to his pain. In a series of images, we see Ian reduced to an animal: masturbating, defecating, laughing and dreaming. 'Weak with hunger,' he eventually devours the baby's corpse and then climbs into a grave that he makes from uprooting the floorboards. Ian's suffering, however, is not yet complete:

> *He dies with relief.*
> *It starts to rain on him, coming through the roof.*
> *Eventually.*
> **Ian** Shit.

Poor Ian can never get any peace. The laughter here comes from the combination of the visual (rain disturbing Ian's repose) and the verbal (his expletive). But it is an uncertain moment. Is Ian dead? The stage direction reads: 'He dies with relief . . . eventually.' On the page, the rain appears to have interrupted that 'eventually'. In performance, Ian's status is even less clear. In the 2001 revival, Ian let out a final groan, as if he was finally passing on, but nothing in the physical reality of the space – the lighting, sound or set – connoted a transition from one world to another. In the 2008 New York production, since the room was already transformed into an 'abstract' space by the blast, what would Ian's death matter anyway, since he was already in another world?

This lack of clarity in text and production suggests that it does not, in fact, matter whether Ian is alive or dead: 'Punish me or rescue me makes no difference,' Ian earlier told Cate. If Cate is vindicated, and there is an afterlife, then Ian's discovery is that it is no better than this world. In death, people are still hungry; people still get wet. If he remains alive, his chance of finally dying 'with relief' has been thwarted by a simple act of nature. In either case, Ian's rain-soaked head uttering 'Shit' produces laughs. Metaphysical comfort is again squashed by the reality of bodily discomfort. It's a good joke, and it is good to be reminded that laughter still exists even in circumstances as extreme as these.

Cate's gift

Following the rain, Cate returns with 'blood seeping between her legs', the result, no doubt, of multiple assaults at the hands of soldiers. But she brings some much-needed supplies: 'some bread, a large sausage and a bottle of gin'. In silence, she feeds Ian, comforting him. Ian's simple response: 'Thank you.' Rain, the sound of which closes the previous three scenes, works as a literal cleansing in the finale. Ian is not dead yet, and during this brief respite the rain soothes his wounds. In performance, the rain literally clears away much of the stage blood on the actor's face, transforming him. More important, Cate has refused to abandon him. In giving him comfort and sustenance, she allows Ian to live, even if just for a little longer, and for that gift, Ian is in her debt. After all that has happened, he must acknowledge that Cate's gesture of food and company is one of insurmountable generosity. But gifts usually have a cost. After Ian 'gives' Cate flowers at the end of Scene One, the next scene opens with the aftermath of Cate's rape. Men might not be able to give freely in *Blasted*, but Cate can. She does not ask for anything in return, no counter-gift, no submission; it is, instead, a pure giving.

Perhaps Kane puts her characters in states of such extreme abjection in order to show how a true gift works. In intense circumstances such as a civil conflict, bodies are shattered, but in the aftermath, and only then, can a person sincerely give without any expectation. The philosopher Jacques Derrida, in his writings about the gift, claims that what a gift gives is the gift of time, and that 'given time' is outside any economic demands: it is the time of freedom and possibility. The time given, in extending Ian's life and by extension Cate's, allows both to start again at ground zero. To borrow Derrida's words, their bodies say, 'we will have to begin all over again' in the light of everything that we have experienced.[62] As *Blasted* vividly demonstrates, a body, following such trauma, becomes open to possibilities hitherto deemed unthinkable. Though perhaps only a god could ever see the body as an empty slate, Kane shows that the scars that her characters bear can bring about change; but it is a process that must be seen. We bear witness to Ian going from rapist to broken man. And in that process of disintegration, the self cannot reproduce the same, thus freeing Ian and Cate from the prison of violence. At the end of *Blasted*, for a brief moment, all debts are cancelled, all wrongs, if only momentarily, are righted. The gift of time demands that Ian, Cate – and, by extension, the audience – rethink their place in this world.

Some (including the author herself) have claimed that this ending is ultimately 'hopeful'. One of the curses of being an American is an infallible sense of optimism, even when events suggest this to be a mistake. As an American, I am not sure I can call *Blasted* a hopeful play. Despite the jokes, there is a lot of suffering that precedes the play's final moments. And watching *Blasted* is an arduous experience. Yet ultimately, it is a play that suggests the possibility that good – though not the Good in any moralistic sense – can emerge from even the bleakest of moments. Some readers might agree with me, while others will find that I am grabbing hold of the barest hint of hope that I can find in this play in order to defend its cruelty. Some might even call it a rather Christian response:

Cate the eternal nurturer sounds, perhaps, a bit Jesus-like. Others might counter that Cate is merely maintaining the expected 'feminine' role as caregiver. I remain optimistic, however. Irrespective of how we read this final moment, we all must concede one thing. Following Ian's 'thank you', Kane's script announces, 'Blackout.' The play is over. Yet it leaves us with the question: what comes next? For Cate and Ian? For us? Only we can answer that question.

Conclusion

What remains exciting about Kane's first play is the challenge that it issues to us – as audience members, as thinkers and as theatre-makers. To playwrights inspired by Kane, how can we create work that is as impactful, as experiential in nature, while still engaging the larger world and the issues that face us all, issues that sometimes feel insurmountable – such as the crisis concerning the environment? To directors and actors who tackle *Blasted*, how do we accomplish the impossible task of performing the things that this script asks of us? To critical thinkers, how can we investigate and challenge the ideas of the play in a way that does not succumb to the knee-jerk responses of its early critics, nor merely read the play through the convenient but ultimately unhelpful lens of biography?

I cannot claim to have adequately answered any of these questions here. These pages are not intended to be the final word, but instead a starting point for future discussions about this challenging and beautiful play. Readers are encouraged to use and abuse the ideas presented here in order to make their own sense of Kane's play. In the spirit of Cate's final act in the play, think of these words as a gift. Now, get to work.

LIBRARY, ░░░░░░░ ░░ ░░░ ░░

Notes to Commentary

I would like to thank Simon Kane, Charlotte Loveridge, Mark Dudgeon, Aleks Sierz, Graham Saunders, Dan Rebellato, Nadine Holdsworth, Elin Diamond, and all my students for the past five years in my 'Contemporary Theatre' seminar at Harvard University. Your advice and questions helped me work through my ideas on Kane. Special thanks to Matthew Kaiser for being my partner in everything.

1 Dan Rebellato, 'Brief Encounter Platform', public interview with Sarah Kane, Royal Holloway, University of London, 3 November 1998.

2 Jack Tinker, review of *Blasted*, *Daily Mail*, 19 January 1995.

3 Charles Spencer, review of *Blasted*, *Daily Telegraph*, 19 January 1995.

4 Michael Billington, review of *Blasted*, *Guardian*, 20 January 1995.

5 Billington, '87 Deadly Sins', *Observer*, 22 November 1994: 5.

6 Benedict Nightingale, *The Future of Theatre*, London: Phoenix, 1998: 27.

7 Billington, *One Night Stands: A Critic's View of Modern British Theatre*, London: Nick Hern, 1993: 360, 361.

8 David Edgar, 'Provocative Acts: British Playwriting in the Post-War Era and Beyond', in *State of Play, Issue One: Playwrights on Playwriting*, ed. David Edgar, London: Faber and Faber, 1999: 19.

9 Review of *Blasted*, *Guardian*, 4 April 2001.

10 Michael Billington, review of *Blasted*, *Guardian*, 29 October 2010 <http://www.guardian.co.uk/stage/2010/oct/29/blasted-by-sarah-kane-review>.

11 Michael Coveney, review of *Blasted*, *Observer*, 5 February 1995.

12 Michael Billington, 'Fabulous Five', *Guardian*, 13 March 1996.

13 Ludwig Wittgenstein, *Philosophical Investigations*, New York: Macmillan, 1958: 32.

14 Quoted in Andrew Calcutt, *Brit Cult: An A–Z of British Pop Culture*, London: Prion Books, 2000: 230–31.

15 Heidi Stephenson and Natasha Langridge, *Rage and Reason: Women Playwrights on Playwriting*, London: Methuen, 1997: 134.

16 Nils Tabert, 'Gespräch mit Sarah Kane', in *Playspotting: Die Londoner Theaterszene der 90er*, ed. Nils Tabert, Reinbeck, 1998: 8–21. My thanks to Graham Saunders for making an unpublished English translation of this interview available to me.

17 Johan Thielemans, 'Interview with Sarah Kane and Vicky Featherstone', *Rehearsing the Future: 4th European Theatre Directors Forum, Strategies for the Emerging Director in Europe*, London, 1999: 13.

18 Sarah Kane, letter to Aleks Sierz, 4 January 1999.

19 See Peter Bürger, *Theory of the Avant-Garde*, trans. Michael Shaw, Minnesota: University of Minnesota Press, 1984.

20 Martin McDonagh, quoted in Sierz, *In-Yer-Face Theatre: Modern Drama Today*, New York and London: Faber and Faber, 2001: 222.

21 Anthony Neilson, quoted in Sierz, *In-Yer-Face Theatre*: 66; Martin McDonagh, quoted in Sierz, *In-Yer-Face Theatre*: 222, 224; Sarah Kane, 'Drama with Balls', *Guardian*, 20 August 1998.

22 Robert Hewison, 'Rebirth of a Nation,' *The Times*, 19 May 1996.

23 David Edgar, 'Provocative Acts: British Playwriting in the Post-War Era and Beyond,' in *State of Play, Issue One: Playwrights on Playwriting*, ed. David Edgar, London: Faber and Faber, 1999: 28.

24 Quoted in John Lloyd, 'Cool Britannia Warms Up', *New Statesman*, 13 March 1998: 10.

25 Interview with Aleks Sierz, 18 January 1999. The specific comment about *Reservoir Dogs* comes from an interview with Rodolfo di Giammarco, 16 September 1997.

26 For more on 1990s theatre and the moment of 'Cool Britannia', see my essay, 'Cruel Britannia', in *Cool Britannia? British Political Drama in the 1990s*, eds. Graham Saunders and Rebecca D'Monté, London: Palgrave, 2007: 38–55.

27 See Dan Rebellato, *1956 And All That: The Making of Modern British Drama*, London and New York: Routledge, 1999.

28 See interview with Aleks Sierz, 18 January 1999; interview with Rodolfo di Giammarco, 16 September 1997; and interview with Graham Saunders, 12 June 1995.

29 Interview with Rodolfo di Giammarco, 16 September 1997.

30 Interview with Aleks Sierz, 18 January 1999.

31 Harold Pinter, 'Writing for the Theatre', *Complete Works: One*, New York: Grove, 1976: 13–14.

32 Interview with Graham Saunders, 12 June 1995.

33 Ibid.

34 Ibid.

35 William Shakespeare, *King Lear*, New York: Signet, 1963: IV.vi.55.

36 For more on the connection between *King Lear* and *Blasted*, see Graham Saunders, ' "Out Vile Jelly": Sarah Kane's *Blasted* and Shakespeare's *King Lear*', *New Theatre Quarterly*, 20:1 (2004): 69–78.

37 See Robert S. Miola, *Shakespeare and Classical Tragedy: The Influence of Seneca*, Oxford and New York: Oxford University Press, 1992; and John Kerrigan, *Revenge Tragedy: Aeschylus to Armageddon*, Oxford and New York: Oxford University Press, 1996, for examples of reading *King Lear* within the tradition of the Jacobean revenge tragedy.

38 Jan Kott, '*King Lear* or *Endgame*', in *Shakespeare Our Contemporary*, trans. Boleslaw Taborski, London: Methuen, 1964: 127.

39 For more on the connection between Barker and Kane, see my article 'An Ethics of Catastrophe: The Theatre of Sarah Kane', *PAJ: A Journal of Performance and Art*, 69 (September 2001): 36–46.

40 Interview with Aleks Sierz, 18 January 1999.

41 The first draft of *Blasted* was completed on 18 April 1993, and does feature Vladek. This was the draft that Kane described as 'full of dense monologues about characters' backgrounds, every feeling was stated, every thought spoken' (interview with Sierz, 18 January 1999). This second draft (June 1993) has the first two scenes of the play that are closer to the final version of the play, and features Vladek in its final pages. An excerpt from this second draft was

staged at Birmingham University's Allardyce Nicoll Studio Theatre on 3 July 1993 as part of the conclusion of Kane's MA degree. The play was staged up to the moment when Ian exclaims 'I Am A Killer', as Cate performs fellatio on him. Thanks to Simon Kane for illuminating the various drafts.

42 When Kane begins the third draft of the play in October 1993, she no longer refers to the Soldier as Vladek.

43 Personal interview with Sean Holmes, 29 November 2010.

44 Personal interview with Louis Cancelmi, 15 June 2010.

45 Personal interview with Sarah Benson, 18 June 2010

46 Personal interview with Sean Holmes, 29 November 2010.

47 Ibid.

48 Samuel Beckett, *Catastrophe*, in *The Collected Shorter Plays of Samuel Beckett*, New York: Grove Press, 1984: 301.

49 Quoted in James Knowlson, *Damned to Fame: The Life of Samuel Beckett*, New York: Grove Press, 1996: 597.

50 Stephenson and Langridge, *Rage and Reason: Women Playwrights on Playwriting*: 131

51 Quoted in Tom Sellar, 'Truth and Dare: Sarah Kane's *Blasted*', *Theater*, 27:1 (1996): 34.

52 Quoted in Simon Hattenstone, 'A Sad Hurrah', *Guardian*, 1 July 2000.

53 Edgar, 'Provocative Acts': 28.

54 Michael Kimmel, 'Masculinity as Homophobia', in *Reconstructing Gender: A Multicultural Anthology*, ed. Estelle Disch, New York: McGraw-Hill, 2002: 104.

55 Kane, *Start the Week*, BBC Radio 4, 20 February 1995, quoted in Graham Saunders, *'Love Me or Kill Me': Sarah Kane and the Theatre of Extremes*, Manchester and New York: Manchester University Press, 2002: 27.

56 Sarah Kane, letter to Aleks Sierz, 18 January 1999.

57 Giles Deleuze, *Negotiations*, New York: Columbia University Press, 1995: 100.

58 Alain Badiou, *Ethics: An Essay on the Understanding of Evil*, London and New York: Verso, 2001: 28

59 Badiou: 47, 52.

60 Samuel Beckett, *Three Novels: Molloy, Malone Dies, The Unnamable*, New York: Grove Press, 1955: 414.

61 Elana Greenfield, 'Kane in Babel: Notes', *The Brooklyn Rail*,
    Dec 2008–Jan 2009.
62 Jacques Derrida, *Given Time, 1. Counterfeit Money*, Chicago
    and London: University of Chicago Press, 1992: 41.
    Derrida is talking about a text by French sociologist Marcel
    Mauss.

Further Reading

Plays by Sarah Kane

Complete Plays, London: Methuen, 2001. (Contains Kane's five stage plays *Blasted*, *Phaedra's Love*, *Cleansed*, *Crave* and *4.48 Psychosis*, and the screenplay for the ten-minute film *Skin*.)

Writing about Kane

Lauren De Vos and Graham Saunders (eds), *Sarah Kane in Context*, Manchester and New York: Manchester University Press, 2010. (A recent collection of essays that examines all Kane's plays including an essay about her early monologues.)

Elana Greenfield, 'Kane in Babel: Notes', *The Brooklyn Rail*, Dec 2008–Jan 2009. (A friend's reflections on Kane's time during her residency at New Dramatists in New York.)

Simon Hattenstone, 'A Sad Hurrah', *Guardian*, 1 July 2000. (An overview of Kane's career on the occasion of the first production of *4.48 Psychosis*.)

Helen Iball, *Sarah Kane's Blasted*, London: Continuum, 2008. (An extended analysis of Kane's first play.)

Elizabeth Kuti, 'Tragic Plots from Bootie to Baghdad', *Contemporary Theatre Review*, Vol. 18, No. 4 (2008): 457–69. (A reading of three plays including Kane's *Blasted* through the lens of Aristotle's definition of tragedy.)

Peter Morris, 'The Mark of Kane', *Areté*, Vol. 4 (2000): 143–52. (An essay on Kane's work and the impact of her death by playwright Morris.)

Dan Rebellato, 'Sarah Kane: An Appreciation', *New Theatre Quarterly*, Vol. 15, No. 59 (2001): 280–81. (A brief appreciation of Kane's career written following her death.)

Graham Saunders, *About Kane: the Playwright & the Work*, London: Faber and Faber, 2009. (A helpful collection of Kane's interviews as well as context about Kane's work.)

————, 'Love Me or Kill Me': Sarah Kane and the Theatre of Extremes. Manchester and New York: Manchester University Press, 2002. (The first book-length study on Kane's work, including readings of all the plays as well as a collection of interviews.)

————, ' "Out Vile Jelly": Sarah Kane's Blasted and Shakespeare's King Lear', New Theatre Quarterly, Vol. 20, No. 1 (2004): 69–78. (An examination of Kane's play in relation to its invocation of Shakespeare's tragedy.)

Tom Sellar, 'Truth and Dare: Sarah Kane's Blasted', Theater 27:1 (1996): 29–34. (A brief overview of Blasted to introduce the publication of the play in the magazine.)

Aleks Sierz, In-Yer Face Theatre: Modern Drama Today, New York and London: Faber and Faber, 2001. (The highly influential study that gave Kane's generation its most enduring name.)

————, 'Still In-Yer-Face?: Towards a Critique and Summation', New Theatre Quarterly, Vol. 18 (February 2002): 17–24. (A reflection on the moment of 'in-yer-face' at the start of the new millennium.)

Annabelle Singer, ' "I Don't Want to Be This": The Elusive Sarah Kane', TDR: The Drama Review, Vol. 48, No. 2 (2004): 139–71. (A personal account of Singer grappling with the issues of Kane's work, focusing on issues of trauma.)

Kim Solga, 'Blasted's Hysteria: Rape, Realism and the Threshold of the Visible', Modern Drama, Vol. 50, No. 3 (2007): 346–74. (A reading of Kane's play that focuses on the implications of Cate's offstage rape.)

Ken Urban, 'An Ethics of Catastrophe: The Theatre of Sarah Kane', PAJ: A Journal of Performance and Art, 69 (September 2001): 36–46. (The first extended article published in the US on Kane's work, looking at the 2001 Kane season at the Royal Court.)

————, 'Cruel Britannia', in Graham Saunders and Rebecca D'Monté (eds), Cool Britannia? British Political Drama in the 1990s, London: Palgrave, 2007: 38–55. (An examination of the politics of the 'in-yer-face' generation in the context of the moment of 'Cool Britannia'.)

————, 'The Body's Cruel Joke: The Comic Theatre of Sarah Kane', in Mary Luckhurst and Nadine Holdsworth (eds), *A Concise Companion to Contemporary British and Irish Drama*, Oxford: Blackwell, 2007: 149–70. (An examination of the role of humour in Kane's plays, with a specific focus on *Blasted* and *Cleansed*.)

Influences

Howard Barker, *Arguments for a Theatre*, Manchester and New York: Manchester University Press, 1997. (A collection of Barker's essays that highly influenced Kane's thinking on drama.)

Samuel Beckett, *The Collected Shorter Plays of Samuel Beckett*, New York: Grove Press, 1984. (A collection of Beckett's shorter plays including *Catastrophe*.)

————, *Endgame and Act Without Words*, New York: Grove Press, 1958.

————, *Waiting for Godot*, New York: Grove Press, 1954.

Edward Bond, *Saved* (student edition), London: Methuen, 2009.

Harold Pinter, *The Essential Pinter: Selections from the Work of Harold Pinter*, New York: Grove Press, 2006. (Contains nine plays from Pinter's career including *One for the Road*, along with a selection of poems and his 2005 Nobel Lecture.)

Acting Exercises

1. A helpful exercise for actors (as well as directors and dramaturgs) is to trace the events of a play backwards to forwards. Write out all of the events of *Blasted*, but start at the end of the play and work your way to the beginning. You can do this as a list. How does mapping the play's chain of events in reverse help you gain a better sense of each of the characters' logic and psychology?

2. Performing explicit acts of sex or violence on stage is not easy, but one way to overcome the initial fear of performing in *Blasted* is to imagine those moments as complicated pieces of blocking or choreography. Choose a 'shocking' moment from the play (for instance, when Cate performs oral sex and then bites Ian's penis at the moment he yells, 'Killer'). Break down that moment into a series of discrete actions. Be as specific as possible. How does it change how you approach the moment?

3. How would you approach the character of the Soldier? What would he sound like? Dress like?

4. What does Cate's laugh sound like? If you were performing that role, what physical changes would Cate undergo during one of her fits?

5. About the characters in *Blasted*, Kane once said: 'All [the actors] need to know is [the characters] don't know why they do it.' As an actor approaching the role of Ian, how can you embrace the fact that sometimes the character is unaware of why he is doing certain actions (for instance, the sexual assault that he carries out on Cate when she is unconscious)? Does it change how you approach such a moment when you view it not as a logical act, but as a moment when the character is driven purely by desire?

6. Marin Ireland, who played Cate in the New York premiere, said this about playing the role: 'The challenge for me has been staying on a simple task. I try to take the burden off myself to communicate the metaphorical poetry of the play. I remember it's not actually my job. I just function within the scene' (*New York Times*, 5 October 2008). What does Ms Ireland mean? How does her comment help you approach the play?

Questions for Further Study

1. Imagine yourself as a representative of the Royal Court Theatre during the initial debates about *Blasted* in January 1995. How would you defend the play against the critics who attacked it?

2. Marin Ireland, the actress who played Cate in the New York production, said this about *Blasted*: 'It is so much, as all of her plays are, about love' (*New York Times*, 5 October 2008). How is the play about the possibility (or impossibility) of love?

3. Describe the dramatic form of *Blasted*. Think about the classical three unities: unity of time (all events to take place during 24 hours), unity of action (one main plot), and unity of place (occurs in one location). How does the play both maintain and subvert these classical unities?

4. Sound plays an important role in *Blasted*. Think about the sound of summer rain, autumn rain, heavy winter rain. Or the sound of the blast in the blackout between Scenes Two and Three. What information is being conveyed by those sounds? As a potential director of the play, how would you talk to a potential sound designer about these moments?

5. How would you describe Ian's journey through the play? Where does he begin? What changes has he undergone by the play's end?

6. Images play an important role in *Blasted*. Choose an image from the play and describe what information it conveys to an audience.

7. The plays of Samuel Beckett strongly influenced Kane's work. What echoes of *Waiting for Godot* and *Endgame* do you find in *Blasted*?

8. Is suffering redemptive in Kane's play? That is, does the suffering that Cate and Ian undergo transform them, heal them, or leave them in a worse state than when the play began?

9. Harold Barker calls his work 'theatre of catastrophe' because it is 'a non-Utopian art which pits cruelty against pity and recognises their coexistence in the guilty and innocent alike' (*Arguments for a Theatre*, p. 122). In what ways is *Blasted* an example of Barker's 'theatre of catastrophe'?

10. Kane said that she thought Cate was 'possibly the most intelligent' of all of the characters in *Blasted*. In what ways is Cate more perceptive than either Ian or the Soldier?

11. How does rape function in *Blasted*? What are the differences and similarities between the various incidents of rape in the play?

12. Some male actors have wondered if Kane's play suggests that all men are potential rapists. Do you think that is what the play is arguing?

13. There is much speculation about what happens to the hotel room when it is 'blasted' by a mortar bomb at the end of Scene Two. How do you read that moment?

14. How do you read the final moment of *Blasted*? What do you make of Cate's return and Ian's 'thank you'? How does the stage picture impact your thinking?

15. Have recent events such as 9/11, the London bombings of 7 July 2005 and the occupation of Iraq changed how we understand *Blasted*?

KEN URBAN is an award-winning playwright and director. His plays include *I ❤ KANT*, *Nibbler*, *Halo*, *The Private Lives of Eskimos*, *The Absence of Weather*, *Sense of an Ending*, *The Female Terrorist Project* and *The Happy Sad*. He is currently working on two new plays, *The Correspondent* and *The Awake*, and a screenplay adaptation of *The Happy Sad*.

In addition to directing his own work, Ken has directed plays by Sarah Kane, Tennessee Williams and Harold Pinter. He also founded The Committee, a New York-based theatre company that produces 'catastrophic theatre', and served as its artistic director from 2002 to 2008.

His critical essays about theatre have appeared in *Performing Arts Journal*, *New Theatre Quarterly*, *Modern Drama*, *Theater*, *Contemporary Theatre Review*, and the anthologies *Cool Britannia? British Political Drama in the 1990s* and *A Concise Companion to Contemporary British and Irish Theatre* . He graduated with honours from Bucknell University and earned his PhD in English Literature at Rutgers University. Ken has taught drama and writing at Rutgers University and Bucknell University. He currently teaches theatre and playwriting at Harvard University.